INSTRUCTIONAL APPLICATIONS OF BEHAVIOR PRINCIPLES

BASIC CONCEPTS IN EDUCATIONAL PSYCHOLOGY SERIES
Larry R. Goulet, University of Illinois, Series Editor

LANGUAGE AND LEARNING
Frank DiVesta, Pennsylvania State University

INSTRUCTIONAL APPLICATIONS OF BEHAVIOR PRINCIPLES
J. Ronald Gentile, State University of New York at Buffalo
Thomas W. Frazier, Behavioral Technology Consultants
Mary C. Morris, Behavioral Technology Consultants

MOTIVATION, PERSONALITY, AND INTELLIGENCE
Kennedy T. Hill, University of Illinois

SOCIOCULTURAL INFLUENCES ON BEHAVIOR AND DEVELOPMENT
Martin L. Maehr, University of Illinois

INSTRUCTIONAL APPLICATIONS OF BEHAVIOR PRINCIPLES

J. RONALD GENTILE
State University of New York at Buffalo

THOMAS W. FRAZIER
MARY C. MORRIS
Behavioral Technology Consultants
Silver Spring, Maryland

BROOKS/COLE PUBLISHING COMPANY
MONTEREY, CALIFORNIA
A Division of Wadsworth Publishing Company, Inc.

ISBN: 0-8185-0092-1
L.C. Catalog Card No: 73-75336
Printed in the United States of America
1 2 3 4 5 6 7 8 9 10—77 76 75 74 73

This book was edited by Anne Phillips and designed by Linda Marcetti. It was typeset by The Heffernan Press, Inc., Worcester, Massachusetts, and printed and bound by Malloy Lithographing, Inc., Ann Arbor, Michigan.

SERIES FOREWORD

The present time marks an exciting period in the history of education. We are reconceptualizing the nature of formal settings in which teaching and learning take place. In addition, we are developing alternative models for teaching and learning. We have rediscovered the importance of the home, parents, and peers in the educational process. And, we are experiencing rapid change and continual advances in the technology of teaching and in the definition of the goals, objectives, and products of education.

The broad concern with the process of education has created new audiences for education-related courses, a demand for new offerings, and the need for increased flexibility in the format for courses. Furthermore, colleges and schools of education are initiating new courses and curricula that appeal to the broad range of undergraduates and that focus squarely on current and relevant social and educational issues.

The Basic Concepts in Educational Psychology series is designed to increase the flexibility of both the instructor and the student. The scope of the series is broad, yet each volume in the series is self-contained and may be used as either a primary or a supplementary text. In addition, the topics for the volumes in the series have been carefully chosen so that several books in the series may be adopted for use in introductory courses or for advanced courses with a specialized focus. Furthermore, each of the volumes is suitable for use in classes operating on the semester or quarter system, or for modular, in-service training, or workshop modes of instruction.

Larry R. Goulet

PREFACE

This book presents a framework for understanding and therefore modifying behavior—specifically behavior that occurs in the special environments designed for instructional purposes. Instructional environments, by definition, are concerned with changing behavior, both cognitive and emotional: increasing reading skill, improving problem-solving strategies, inducing positive attitudes toward various ethnic groups, and so on. In the daily process of instructional changes, the students themselves, their teachers, their administrators, their parents, and others all interact and influence one another's subsequent behaviors. The complexity of their behavior cannot be overestimated, but neither should it be allowed to overwhelm us. Much is known about the effects of environments on behavior; this knowledge can be applied to instructional environments to improve the conditions of both students and teachers. Such application and improvement is the purpose of this book.

This book is an appropriate text for undergraduate or graduate students who want to see the application of psychological principles to such instructional problems as motivation and discipline and for in-service or pre-service teachers. No previous background in psychology is assumed. However, students already familiar with the principles may still find the applications useful, as we have found to be the case in our own courses.

This text is organized into seven chapters, each of which is preceded by a list of study questions. The study questions can be considered instructional objectives in the sense that, if you know the answer to each of the questions, you have attained the objective—that is, you have learned the material that this text was designed to teach. For the student, therefore, the best use of the text would probably be to refer to the study questions often, including returning to them at the conclusion of the chapter to assure your mastery of the concepts and principles presented. For the instructor, the best use of the text would probably be to assess in some way whether each student has achieved the instructional objectives specified by the study questions.

We have also included an Appendix, which is a checklist meant to suggest the type of questions that teachers should ask themselves about their use of the principles of this text. The questions do not exhaust our subject, but they are representative of the major points made throughout the book. We hope that by using these questions (the type of questions that a behaviorist might ask about the structure and functioning of a classroom), you will find a practical and useful summary of the principles you have studied.

In addition to the Appendix, we have included a Glossary to assist you in learning the new terminology introduced in the book.

An earlier version of this book (Frazier, Gentile, & Morris, 1970) was employed in several educational psychology courses, ranging in size from 40 to 300 students. The general procedures used in those courses, which were quite favorably received by both the staff and students (Gentile, 1971b), have been derived from the principles in this book. They are close relatives of, and indeed were influenced by, procedures reported by Keller (1968) and Ferster and Perrott (1968).

We would like to express our appreciation to reviewers Robert T. Filep of the Institute for Educational Development, El Segundo, and Larry R. Goulet and Warren Steinman of the University of Illinois, Urbana. In addition, we want to thank Fred S. Keller of Western Michigan University; Billie H. Frazier of the University of Maryland; Patricia K. Gentile of Amherst, New York; Claudia Lee of the State University of New York, Buffalo; and the proctors and students in the courses in which these materials have been used for their ideas, encouragement, and hard work at various stages in the preparation of this text. Thanks are also due to Lorelei Sklar, Jackie Rance, Dian Jensen, and Mildred Coho for their secretarial assistance beyond the call of duty.

J. Ronald Gentile
Thomas W. Frazier
Mary Carolyn Morris

CONTENTS

INSTRUCTIONAL APPLICATIONS OF BEHAVIOR PRINCIPLES

INTRODUCTION

As the first phase of her student-teaching experience, a young teacher was observing her supervising teacher conduct high school English classes. As she described it, each 47-minute class period began with what she labeled the "search-and-deposit" mission: "Wrap that gum up in paper. Don't throw it naked into the basket." The supervising teacher was searching for gum chewers, who, in addition to having to deposit their gum in full view of the rest of the class, were required to pay a fee of 5 cents (used to purchase facial tissues for the students to use or to buy get-well cards for classmates). What was alarming to the new teacher was the amount of time this procedure took—an average of 15 minutes per class when the topic was grammar and an average of 5 minutes per class when the topic was literature. (Interestingly, the supervising teacher had mentioned that students liked literature but did not like grammar.)

What was perceived immediately by the student teacher, and evidently overlooked by the experienced teacher, was that the students enjoyed this game and were willing to pay the small fine in order to keep the teacher from beginning class. In other words, the teacher was actually rewarding the behavior she sought to punish, and by so doing she was increasing rather than decreasing the incidence of that behavior.

This of course is not an isolated incident. Girls wear miniskirts and boys grow their hair long as soon as the school or their parents impose rules disallowing such behavior. In fact, a very successful play, *The Fantasticks,* was developed around the idea that children will want to do whatever it is that is forbidden. The phenomenon is so widespread that experienced observers can state it as a general rule of classroom behavior: *those behaviors that receive the teacher's most concerned and genuine interest are those that occur with the highest frequency.*

The student teacher understood this, and, when she took control of the class, she purposely ignored gum chewing and directed her attention to task-oriented behaviors. Beginning on two literature days, she carefully planned a strategy to engage the students in a discussion she could maintain for some time. Though there was gum chewing, she ignored it. On the third day, grammar day, came the real test. In her words:

> On Monday almost everyone was chewing gum and the chewing was more vigorous. All those chomping jaws seemed to be saying . . . NOTICE ME . . . NOTICE ME . . . NOTICE ME. What a ghastly sight! As my breakfast churned in my stomach, I was determined not to respond to the gum chewing. After a few minutes, a student asked if I liked to chew gum. My reply was no. Then he wanted to know why I hadn't done anything about the gum chewing. I replied that obviously it was a waste of time since gum chewing did not decrease. We did spend a few minutes discussing why gum chewing was undesirable in an English class. The class agreed that as discussion became more heated and students became excited it was difficult to understand the speaker if gum was being chewed.
>
> At this point I introduced a contingency. Grammar was an unpopular activity. As a reward for completing the grammar activities, the class could discuss topics of interest to them, such as movies, music, television shows, cartoons, performers, and current happenings.*

Gum chewing did not cease instantly, but the student teacher continued to ignore it, spending the time usefully to encourage the students to complete the assignments. In the presence of the supervising teacher, the class often did not complete the assignments, while under the student teacher's procedure, "the students worked efficiently and rapidly to finish the grammar lessons." Of equal (and maybe more) importance, the student teacher found the extra time for free discussions an excellent way to get to know the students, their interests, and their needs.

A whole range of problems—from the relatively harmless example of gum chewing to extremely harmful examples of head-banging and other self-mutilating and violent behaviors—can often be substantially altered by seemingly simple shifts of attention on the part of a significant other person such as a parent or teacher. The shift-of-attention solution to problems is often viewed as only common sense when pointed out to many people. This is why we used the words "seemingly simple." If it *were* common sense, these problems would not be so common.

One of the authors once had a student who complained that our emphasis on attention to appropriate behaviors instead of punishment for inappropriate behaviors was only common sense. She was in the habit of bringing her dog to class, and, as luck would have it, shortly after she complained about the "common-sense" nature of the principle, her dog did not obey one of her commands. What she did was go over and kick the dog. It seems ironic that her "common-sense" notion of training her dog

* Margaret L. Zabranskey (unpublished, 1970). Reprinted by permission.

was based more on punishment for inappropriate behavior than on praise for the desired behavior.

No, common sense alone is not sufficient to analyze these common problems and develop solutions. What is required is an ability to analyze the environmental conditions that serve to maintain behaviors in the first place. To provide such an ability is the purpose of this book.

Before we discuss the basic principles of what is often called the experimental analysis of behavior, a word on the *flavor* of these principles is in order. At times, the principles are presented as though they can be applied and will work as described in an entirely mechanistic, automatic manner. In some cases they will be effective if applied in this manner. However, professionals in this field seldom, if ever, apply the principles mechanistically. Instead, they apply them with a genuine, unconditional, positive regard (an apt phrase of Carl Rogers) for their subjects. Thus, if we talk about giving attention as a reward for some appropriate behavior, we are not talking about giving a mechanistic smile or coldly saying "that's right"; on the contrary, *giving attention should be interpreted as the honest concern that one person has for another person's well-being.* Cold, impersonal attention is not something people seek, and it will seldom, therefore, be rewarding. But honest, warm regard for another person's well-being—whether it be for his health and safety, for his learning, or for his happiness—is sought for and is rewarding. If you keep this in mind as you read the rest of the text, the objective manner of presenting the principles will be placed in the proper perspective—that of a helping relationship.

When first introduced to principles of behavior analysis, even within the helping-relationship context, some people think that it smacks of control and manipulation by an external authority. In this regard, the management of behavior by the principles in this book is *not an invention* by behaviorists. The behavior management we propose is, rather, the *effective use* of principles that operate daily in our lives to control our behavior. We seldom analyze our daily lives in this way; but when we do, it becomes obvious how behavior is controlled by its consequences. For example, if you have a bad experience dating a particular person, you are unlikely to date him again. On the other hand, a person who treats you nicely is likely to be one you like. A child who succeeds in sports or reading is likely to continue, while the one who is ridiculed is likely to give up more easily. In other words, the consequences of our behaviors determine to a great extent our future willingness to engage in such behaviors.

Thus the question for someone (such as a teacher) who is charged with helping someone else is not *whether* to control behavior but whether the control should be *accidental* or *planned.* Since a teacher's mission is to help each child progress in some specified way during some period of time, planning is essential. Thus planning the consequences of behaviors is a logical part of the teaching-helping process.

Another reason for careful concern with behavioral analysis is that it is necessary to understand the teacher's as well as the student's behavior. A teacher, in other words, is not only the controller of the classroom environment; he is also controlled by the environment. Thus the teacher is likely to discontinue methods that lead to ridicule or boredom on the part of the students. Similarly, he is apt to continue to use techniques that students enjoy or seem to learn from best. Thus the teacher's joys and frustrations—as well as the students'—are tied up in mutual interaction. One cannot be understood in the absence of the other. In general terms, the procedures we advocate are based on the following principles, which are central to any effective instructional process.

1. First, a detailed specification of the objectives (in the form of study questions) is given for each assignment.
2. The material is structured into a hierarchy in which each successive step builds on prerequisite concepts.
3. Each student progresses through each set of materials at his own rate.
4. Student learning is assessed by criterion-referenced methods—that is, each student masters each set of objectives to a pre-established criterion and is not compared with other students.
5. Students receive immediate feedback on the mastery tests.
6. If a student has not learned, the instructor has not taught. In this case, the student is tutored by various means, asked to restudy, and given other opportunities to demonstrate his knowledge of the concepts. Until the student has mastered the concepts, he is considered in the process of learning, with no stigma attached.
7. Students see a working model of the principles taught.

We recommend such procedures in teaching these concepts. Careful behavioral analysis, such as described in this book, can help a teacher understand his own as well as his students' behavior in a classroom.

CHAPTER ONE BEHAVIORAL ANALYSIS

STUDY QUESTIONS

1. Why do different observers often give conflicting acccunts of an event?
2. How can amount of agreement among different observers be increased? What is meant by objectivity?
3. Define the following:
   a. response.
   b. stimulus.
   c. operant.
   d. respondent.
4. What is meant by the rate or frequency of a response?
5. What is the base rate?
6. What is meant by time sampling?
7. In the time-sampling problem of Pete's verbal interruptions:
   a. why was the base rate expressed as some number of verbal interruptions per 50-minute class period?
   b. could the base rate have been expressed in terms of some other period of time? Explain.
   c. of what use will a chart be for evaluating Pete's progress several weeks later?

DEFINITION OF THE PROBLEM

Teachers are often overheard lamenting, "I cannot reach that child," "He is not motivated," or "I cannot control that class." Each of these statements reflects the same basic concern—a concern about how to arrange environmental conditions in such a way that the child can be reached, motivated, or controlled.

The critical phrase for us is *to arrange the environmental conditions.* Whatever else teachers control in a classroom, they do have control over environmental conditions. Fortunately, as will be demonstrated, this control is sufficient to change or maintain behaviors that are of significant importance to the teacher. Such behaviors fall under the rubrics of discipline, interest, and motivation and appear to account for most of the problem behaviors of concern to new teachers.

The fact that behavior is under some environmental control is not a new idea, of course; the whole idea of education is based on it. Educators believe that if a student is exposed to certain materials, he will interact with the environment, learning the material, changing his attitudes, and so on. Nevertheless, recognition of the importance of environmental conditions and the efficient and beneficial use of such conditions are two different matters. Thus, while every teacher controls motivation and discipline in some manner, most teachers use aversive measures as the primary means of controlling behavior: for example, "If you don't behave, you are going to the principal," "If you don't do your homework, you receive an F." Within every classroom, however, is the potential for reversing such negative controls.

The first step in understanding behavior is to describe it accurately. This is often more difficult than it seems to be on the surface, and thus it is necessary to begin our analysis of behavior with a discussion on observational technique.

OBSERVING BEHAVIOR

Behavior can often be carefully observed by several onlookers, yet each will present a different account of the event. These differences in reports can occur for several reasons. Each individual may have been looking at different aspects of the behavior that occurred. Behavior, even of a single individual, is much too complex to allow notation of everything that happens over a period of time. For instance, there are several levels of analysis of human events possible, and many of these are going on simultaneously; muscle tensions, body positions, physiological processes, and verbal behaviors are a few of the observable behaviors that could be recorded at any given time.

Thus observation always has to be highly selective. Another reason for discrepancies in reporting is that inexperienced observers often are highly influenced by their own background and needs. They tend to project their own attitudes or interests into the situation rather than focus on the actual behavior that occurred. This is called *bias*.

To take a familiar example, an 8-year-old makes a sarcastic

remark in an unpleasant tone of voice to his parents. Mother decides that the boy's "nasty streak" is coming out because of his anger about something. She decides to ignore the statement because her past history of dealing with situations like this has convinced her that peace is best kept by not making an issue out of it. Father, however, concludes on the basis of his past experiences with this situation that the boy's behavior occurred because of lack of sleep, and thus he sends him immediately to bed. While these two analyses and solutions are not mutually exclusive, they are colored by each parent's perceptions of the present situation in interaction with their recollections of past behaviors and their own needs of the moment. For example, the father may have been interested in getting the son to bed early so the parents could have some time alone. In fact, the boy may have been trying to get the attention of his parents through peaceful means for the previous hour. But being thwarted by his parents' personal interaction, he became frustrated and reacted angrily. If this were the case, other solutions to cope with the son's disruptive behavior would have been more appropriate. In any case, the attempted solution was based on the unique analysis of the problem by the mother and father. For the parents to agree on a solution, they have to be able to agree on the definition of the problem.

If high degrees of agreement have to be reached among two or more observers regarding the behavior they see, the observers have to be provided with a set of specific categories of behaviors to be observed. In addition, the observers have to be trained and practiced in making the exact kinds of measurements required, including writing observations in simple factual language or according to a coding system.

All of the preceding points about observing, categorizing, and agreeing on behavior can be summarized in the general concept of objectivity. **Objectivity** is an expression of facts with the minimum amount of distortion, prejudice, and interpretation. An objective account of behavior is one in which the facts are presented as accurately as possible, without attempting to guess motives or causes of the behavior. Reports that are objective allow the most agreement from one observer to another, because only behaviors that can be clearly seen or heard and counted are used. Therefore an objective report can be confirmed by another observer as long as the same kind of measurements are used.

Learning to make objective descriptions is one of the basic skills critical to successful use of behavior-modification techniques. The skill is an essential part of the process of analyzing behavior because behavioral data furnish the basis for all decisions.

DESCRIBING BEHAVIOR

RESPONSE: THE UNIT OF BEHAVIOR

Since it would be impossible to perceive or describe everything that someone does, even over a brief period of time, it is necessary to deal with small units or categories of behavior. These categories are called responses and are the basic units used to describe behavior. A **response** is defined as a single act of the organism that is a single operation. This act may be as simple as an eye blink or an eye movement. On the other hand, more complex operations such as walking, talking, or crying may also be called responses, despite the fact that they themselves consist of simpler acts.

All responses occur at some rate or frequency, and the **rate or frequency of a response** is a description of how often that response occurs in some period of time. Thus one worker on an assembly line might place bolts on a piece of machinery at the rate of 15 per minute, whereas the worker opposite him on the line doing the same job might perform at the rate of 25 per minute. The two workers doing the same jobs are observed as working at different rates—that is, the frequency of their responses per minute differs by 10 responses.

In a similar manner, all responses occur at some rate, whether they are breathing responses, study responses, or swearing responses. Many responses are a problem to teachers because they occur at too high a rate in situations when the response is undesirable (such as swearing, interrupting, or throwing chalk in the classroom); thus the problem for the teacher is to reduce the rate of such behaviors. Other responses occur at too low a rate (such as studying or paying attention); in these cases, the problem for the teacher is to increase the rate of the response.

STIMULUS: THE UNIT OF THE ENVIRONMENT

A **stimulus** is an environmental event or occurrence to which an individual or animal is sensitive. Examples are lights, sounds, smells, verbalizations (such as questions and statements), and physical objects (such as people, animals, food, and toys). Although most environmental events are potential stimuli, we are usually only concerned with those stimuli that have some effect on behavior. Responses are usually made because of stimuli, and the rate of the response can depend on the presentation of the stimulus.

OPERANTS AND RESPONDENTS

Some stimuli are presented before responses and are responsible for *eliciting* responses on almost every occasion in which they are presented. Responses elicited or caused in this way are called **respondents,** examples of which are reflexes, such as an eye blink elicited by a puff of air or salivation caused by food in the mouth. The frequency of a respondent is closely associated with the rate at which the eliciting stimulus occurs.

Other stimuli control responses, even though they follow the responses. For example, a faucet handle is turned (the response) in order to obtain water (the stimulus), the television is turned on (the response) to see the show (the stimulus). Such responses are generally called *purposeful behaviors:* we turn the faucet because we want a drink of water. Purposeful behaviors are called **operants** because they operate on the environment to obtain the stimulus. However, the rate of this operant is determined by its consequence—that is, by what kind of stimulus follows the response. In other words, the consequence (water) is the stimulus that follows the response (turning the spigot). If the response has the consequence of obtaining water, then the response may be made again. If, however, the response is not followed by water on several successive occasions, then you become less likely to turn the spigot. In this way the response is controlled by its consequences.

BASE RATES AND TIME SAMPLING

Prerequisite to changing the frequency with which a response occurs, it is necessary to obtain a crucial measurement called the base rate. The **base rate** or **baseline** of a response is a measure of the naturally occurring frequency of a response in some period of time before any attempt has been made to change the response. The base rate provides the data that allow evaluation of any program for changing response rates. Thus, before any attempt is made to change any behavior, either by increasing or decreasing its rate, the base rate of that response should be obtained. Then the rate of the response after the improvement program can be compared with the base rate that existed before the program began.

One way to obtain a base rate of some response would be to count all of the instances of the response throughout the day every day for several weeks. The count thus obtained divided by the number of hours observed would give a frequency per hour of the actual rate of the response. While such a count would be complete, it is totally impractical for classroom applications. What is needed is an *estimate* of the base rate, a measure that is easy to obtain, relatively free from observer bias, and reliable. Such a measure can be obtained by a technique known as time sampling.

Time sampling is a way of observing selected aspects of behavior within uniform and short time intervals. One of the first steps is to define precisely the response that is to be observed and counted, a response often called the *target behavior*. Then a schedule of observation intervals is established. For example, the observer may decide to count all of the target-behavior occurrences between 5 and 10 minutes past the hour every hour of the day in which the particular student of concern is in class. In practice, a teacher is usually only concerned with a few behaviors of a few children at any one time, and these can be dealt with one at a time in this manner. Often, because of the difficulty of attending to more than one behavior at a time, a teacher should plan to solve one problem before dealing with the next.

The schedule of observation periods is established ahead of time to reduce bias. If a strict schedule were not set up, observers would have a tendency to begin counting instances of the target behavior only when they were occurring, and a reliable estimate of the base rate would not be possible. The length, spacing, and number of time intervals should be chosen to provide a representative sampling of an individual's target behavior. It is assumed that, if observations are made systematically over several days or weeks, a fair estimate of the frequency of the individual's response will be observed and documented.

A SAMPLE PROBLEM

Suppose, for example, you are interested in determining the base rate of Pete's verbal interruptions in class, with the ultimate objective of reducing the rate of such interruptions (procedures for changing the rate of responses will be explained later). Since you have more important things to do all day long than count his every instance of this response, you need an accurate estimate of the baseline frequency. So you choose the time-sampling procedure and set up a chart (see Table 1).

This chart constitutes the sample of responses to be obtained twice a day for one week and allows quick tallies of the number of responses. In addition, since you have specified the observational time intervals to cover most of the 50-minute period in which this child is in your class, your sample of responses should be fairly representative and unbiased. Sampling various time intervals prevents getting a biased estimate due to some idiosyncratic circumstance that may be present at a given time each day.

Table 1. Time-sampling data sheet.

Student: Pete Behavior: Verbal interruptions
Age: 13 Observer: Mrs. Jones
Class: History

Time intervals	Frequency	Daily 10-min. total	Estimated daily 50-min. total
Mon. Feb. 2:			
1:05-1:10	111 = 3	9	45
1:30-1:35	~~1111~~ 1 = 6		
Tues. Feb. 3:			
1:15-1:20	= 0	2	10
1:40-1:45	11 = 2		
Wed. Feb. 4:			
1:05-1:10	1111 = 4	7	35
1:35-1:40	111 = 3		
Thurs. Feb. 5:			
1:20-1:25	= 0	0	0
1:30-1:35	= 0		
Fri. Feb. 6:			
1:00-1:05	~~1111~~ 11 = 7	12	60
1:45-1:50	~~1111~~ = 5		
Totals		30	150

$$\text{Base rate per 50-minute period} = \frac{\text{Estimated weekly total}}{\text{Number of days observed}} = \frac{150}{5}$$

$$= \text{30 verbal interruptions per 50-minute class period}$$

With this clear definition and the time-sampling chart, you are now ready to collect baseline data. Class should go on as usual, and no one should know that you are counting responses. Thus, on Monday at 1:05, you simply begin to keep track of the number of target responses made by Pete, either by using some mechanical counting device, by making a mark on the data sheet, or by making mental notes to be recorded at the earliest convenient moment. This procedure is continued until 1:10, at which point counting is stopped. During this time, you may have counted three instances of Pete verbally interrupting, which are recorded on the data sheet.

At 1:30, you go through the same procedure again, and the number of times Pete verbally interrupts is entered on the data sheet. Continuing this procedure twice a day for a full week gives a total of 30 verbal interruptions for the week.

Since the base rate is the naturally occurring frequency of a response in some specified period of time, you need to decide a reasonable time period to use. A 50-minute class period seems reasonable, since it is a natural class unit. Thus the daily 10-minute totals are translated into estimated daily 50-minute totals by multiplying by 5. These values are shown in the last column of the data sheet (see Table 1). The average of those estimated daily 50-minute totals is obtained by summing them and dividing by the number of days on which observations were made. Thus $150/5 = 30$ verbal interruptions per 50-minute class period—a rather large number.

When you begin your program to reduce the frequency of verbal interruptions, this figure of 30 verbal interruptions per 50-minute class will be the baseline against which progress can be measured. In addition to calculating the average number of target responses per unit time, it is often useful to plot the response frequencies on a chart, as we did in Figure 1. Even more useful than the daily chart might be a weekly chart of the average base rates; either chart allows instant evaluation of the student's, as well as your program's, progress.

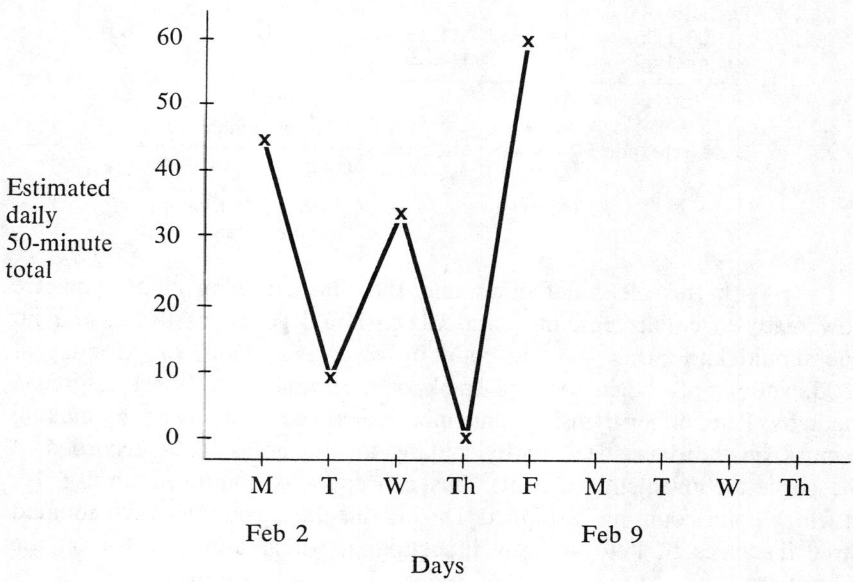

Figure 1. Pete's daily verbal interruptions.

CHAPTER TWO
INCREASING THE FREQUENCY OF A RESPONSE: CONDITIONING AND REINFORCEMENT

STUDY QUESTIONS

1. Describe the procedure used to condition a respondent—that is, describe how a previously neutral stimulus can be brought to elicit a respondent.
2. Describe the way in which respondent conditioning may provide the procedure for learning conditioned emotional responses. Give examples of how a positive and a negative emotional response can be conditioned.
3. In Pavlov's classical-conditioning experiment, identify:
   a. the unconditioned stimulus (US).
   b. the conditioned stimulus (CS).
   c. the conditioned response (CR).
4. Contrast the following in terms of their procedures and their effects on behavior. Give examples.
   a. positive reinforcement.
   b. negative reinforcement.
   c. punishment.
5. Describe the procedure used to condition an operant.
6. Define *reinforcing stimulus*.
7. What is extinction? How does it differ from conditioning?
8. How do the following affect reinforcement effectiveness?
   a. type of reinforcement.
   b. quantity of reinforcement.
   c. delay of reinforcement.
9. What is a reinforcement contingency?
10. Why are reinforcement contingencies important in changing behavior? What is wrong with noncontingent reinforcement? Relate noncontingent reinforcement to superstitious behavior.
11. How does the deprivation-satiation history affect reinforcement effectiveness?
12. What is the difference between primary and secondary reinforcers?
13. How could a secondary reinforcer lose its reinforcing value?
14. Describe the following three types of secondary reinforcers:
    a. social reinforcers.

   b. tokens.
   c. activities.
15. What is the Premack principle governing the use of activities as reinforcers?
16. What is meant by the "emotional effects" of reinforcers?
17. Describe the steps Hall, Lund, and Jackson followed to increase study behaviors in a classroom.
18. Using the general program for increasing response rates as a guide, devise a program to increase or maintain a desirable response in a classroom situation in which you are likely to be involved.

TWO WAYS OF INCREASING THE FREQUENCY OF A RESPONSE

Conditioning is a procedure in which an increase in the frequency of a response occurs as a result of the influence of the presentation of an associated stimulus. There are two basic conditioning procedures (after Skinner, 1938) used to increase the frequency of responses: (1) classical, respondent, or Pavlovian conditioning, in which the frequency of respondents is increased by conditioning, and (2) operant or instrumental conditioning, in which the frequency of operants is increased by conditioning.

RESPONDENT CONDITIONING

For most of us, the experience of going to the dentist provides a real example of respondent conditioning. The sights, sounds, and smells previously associated with the pain of drilling and pulling teeth have become sufficient to cause us to have sweaty palms, changes in blood pressure and heart rate, increased muscle tension, and general restlessness. These physiological changes may occur as soon as we enter the office and may continue to grow stronger the closer we get to the actual drilling. Moreover, the changes usually occur despite our conscious efforts to whistle a happy tune or act brave. How did we come to have these emotional reactions to previously neutral stimuli such as a dentist, his chair, his drill, or the odor of his toothpaste? The best available answer is that we learned to react through the pairing of these neutral stimuli with the actual pain stimuli produced by drilling. The pain, of course, elicits the changes in blood pressure, muscle tension, and so on (respondents) that we described earlier. By the natural co-occurrence of neutral stimuli with pain stimuli, these physiological respondents can come to be elicited by the neutral stimuli. We shall describe this process more systematically.

In classical conditioning we begin with a stimulus (such as meat) that elicits some natural and relatively automatic response (for example, a reflex such as salivation). This stimulus is called an **unconditioned stimulus** because it reliably elicits the response before conditioning is ever begun. The response elicited by the unconditioned stimulus is called an **unconditioned response** or a respondent because it naturally results, like a reflex, when the stimulus is present.

Classical conditioning is a procedure used to bring the respondent under the control of a neutral stimulus—one that could not previously elicit the response. This neutral stimulus (such as the sound of a bell), once it comes to elicit the response, is called a **conditioned stimulus.**

While in the process of studying basic digestive processes (which study won him a Nobel prize), Pavlov (1927) demonstrated classical conditioning in much the way we have described it. Pavlov sounded a tuning fork immediately before placing meat powder in a dog's mouth. The meat powder (the unconditioned stimulus) elicited a salivation response (the respondent or unconditioned response). After a number of presentations of meat powder preceded by the tuning fork, the sound of the tuning fork alone made the dog salivate. In other words, the previously neutral stimulus, the tuning fork's sound, had become a conditioned stimulus: it elicited salivation even though meat powder was no longer presented.

CONDITIONED AVERSION

Since Pavlov's first demonstration, there have been repeated investigations of the effects of his basic procedure for producing conditioned respondents on many species of animals, including man, and for many different types of reflex responses. One of the most famous of these studies (Watson & Rayner, 1920) demonstrated that conditioned emotional reactions could be produced by pairing a neutral stimulus with an aversive unconditioned stimulus. In this study a white rat was placed before an infant named Albert, who was at first attracted to the animal. Then, on successive trials, introduction of the rat into the room was immediately followed by a loud noise. Parents will attest to the fact that a sudden loud noise causes a startle reflex and fear response in an infant, and that was the effect the loud noise had on Albert. In only a few more pairings of the rat with the loud noise, the previously attractive white rat had become a negative and unattractive stimulus that caused a fear response. That is, the white rat had become a conditioned stimulus for a fear response.

What we typically consider a fear response has both respondent and operant components. For example, shouting for help or running away from the fear-producing stimulus are operant components. However, we are presently describing the respondent components of fear—that is, the physiological reflexes that occur mostly without our awareness. Examples of physiological reflexes elicited by painful or other aversive stimuli are changes in heart rate, blood pressure, breathing rate, muscle tension, pupil dilation, palm sweating, and hormone secretions into the blood. These changes are natural biological reflexes to prepare the organism to deal with external threats. As such, they are respondents that also obey the laws of respondent conditioning, which means that they can be conditioned to occur to previously neutral stimuli. Thus we can understand that the white rat, by being paired with an unconditioned stimulus for fear respondents, could come to elicit these same fear respondents.

That an organism is equipped with a mechanism for transferring physiological respondents from unconditioned stimuli to neutral stimuli in this manner is, of course, very adaptive for his survival. Nevertheless, this same mechanism is responsible for the fear of stimuli that have only by chance been paired with the actual unconditioned stimuli. The white rat in Albert's case was only incidentally related to the loud noise; it certainly did not produce the noise, and so Albert had no objective reason to fear it. But such is the nature of classical conditioning. *There need be no causal relationship between the conditioned and unconditioned stimuli; all that is necessary for conditioning to occur is that the conditioned stimulus precede or occur simultaneously with the unconditioned stimulus so that they are perceived as related.*

Moreover, conditioning does not require very many pairings of neutral and unconditioned stimuli to establish reliable fear respondents to the previously neutral stimulus. In one study (Gentile & Lawson, 1969), college-student volunteers were exposed to a series of words, some of which were followed by an electric shock to the leg. For most of these students, three or four word-shock pairings were sufficient to produce a reliably larger galvanic skin response (a measure of electrical conductivity of the palm associated with perspiration changes) to the shocked words than to the nonshocked words.

The rate at which conditioned fears are formed and their final strength depend on the magnitude or severity of the aversive stimulus used. What is important to realize at this point is the apparent ease with which these conditioned fear respondents are formed in situations that involve aversive stimuli (such as punishment or threats of punishment). Moreover, the effects of these conditioned fears are not confined to the conditioned stimulus alone but often *generalize* to other similar stimuli, as we will describe in detail in a later chapter. Not only did Albert learn to fear the white rat, but this fear was generalized so that it was elicited by other furry objects as well (for example, a rabbit and a fur coat).

It is relatively easy to apply these ideas to common situations to provide an explanation for the gut feelings we experience in common threatening situations. The dentist's drill, white coat, and antiseptic odor can indeed become conditioned stimuli for the fear respondents elicited by the pain of drilling teeth. Similarly, a teacher, the subject matter she teaches, and her school room can become conditioned stimuli for fear respondents that were originally produced by harsh punishment from the teacher. Exposure to such conditions can lead, in extreme cases, to neurotic anxiety reactions and phobias and, in more normal cases, to the white knuckles and uneasy stomach most of us experience in the dentist's chair or when presented with difficult mathematical problems.

CONDITIONED ATTRACTION

It is less easy, though probably just as accurate, to explain more positive emotions in a similar way. It is less easy because studies of positive affects are not so easy to design as those involving pain and fear and also because it probably takes longer to condition positive than negative emotions.[1] A prototype of the conditioning of these positive feelings can be imagined by the reduced stomach contractions and general relaxation that result from the ingestion of food when you are hungry. If the food (as an unconditioned stimulus) elicits those feelings of contentment in a reflexive fashion, then it would follow that other concurrent stimuli (such as a mother or a restaurant) could acquire the capacity to elicit those feelings of contentment. Similarly, a spouse or date who is associated with romantic or sexually satisfying feelings of contentment could be expected to elicit such emotions in the future, as might other concurrent events, such as a particular perfume or a song.

These speculations into the influences of conditioning on the everyday lives of people are not meant to suggest that human emotions can be totally explained in this way. Love, hate, and the other affective seasonings of life are much too complicated to be simplistically reduced to respondent conditioning. On the other hand, to ignore the influence of respondent conditioning in the development of emotions is to misunderstand a large part of life.

[1] In fact, we know of no clearly demonstrated conditioning of a positive affect, such as contentment or love, though there are good reasons for expecting it to occur in this manner (for example, Mowrer, 1960).

EXTINCTION

Pavlov found that his dog continued to salivate to the tuning fork as long as there was some periodic presentation of food. If, however, food was discontinued, the dog soon learned that there was no longer an association between tuning fork and food, and eventually it stopped salivating to the tuning fork. This procedure—presenting the conditioned stimulus but withholding the unconditioned stimulus—is technically called *experimental extinction* or, simply, **extinction.** For most conditioned respondents, the procedure of extinction will reduce the frequency of the respondent to near zero, though the process sometimes takes a large number of presentations of the conditioned stimulus in the absence of the unconditioned stimulus. Of course, the longer the habit has been established, the longer the extinction process will take.

In addition, it is a curious phenomenon that it often takes longer to eliminate a response than to condition it, especially a fear response. In fact, for some strong fear responses, it may be impossible to eliminate the response by extinction, since the person will not remain in the vicinity of the conditioned stimulus long enough to find out whether or not the unconditioned stimulus will follow. In one case, the parents of a girl who had an extreme school phobia (fear of school) tried to carry her into the school, as recommended by a mental-health professional. The school was so stressful, however, that the girl passed out when she entered the building. Since there was no way to have the girl attend to conditioned stimuli in the school while she was unconscious, extinction could not be applied. More common examples include abnormal fears of water or height (through traumatic experiences) or extreme dislikes for certain foods. In such extreme cases, procedures such as desensitization and counterconditioning have to be used. (Since we are concerned here with normal behaviors, these procedures are beyond the scope of this book; the interested reader may refer to Reese, 1966, for an introductory account or to Bandura, 1969, for a detailed treatment.) We will discuss other effects of extinction and punishment later.

OPERANT CONDITIONING

In operant or instrumental conditioning, we begin with a response for which we may be able to find no stimulus. Many human behaviors, especially those behaviors we call purposeful, appear to occur without being elicited by some unconditioned stimulus. In these cases, conditioning can occur by presenting the stimulus after the desired response, rather than before it.

The response is called an operant because it operates on the environment. In turn, the consequence of that behavior—that is, the stimulus that follows the operant response—determines whether the same kind of response will (a) increase in frequency, (b) be maintained at the same rate, or (c) reduce in frequency.

POSITIVE REINFORCEMENT

If a response is followed by presentation of a stimulus and the response rate increases or is maintained, the stimulus is called a **reinforcing stimulus.** The presentation of a reinforcing stimulus to increase or maintain the rate or frequency of behavior is called **positive reinforcement;** in other words, the response has been reinforced (which is similar to saying it was rewarded).

For example, if food is presented to a hungry animal after he presses a bar and the rate of the bar-pressing either stays the same or increases, food is called a reinforcing stimulus. If the rate of bar-pressing decreases, food could not be said to be reinforcing. In other words, *a stimulus can be said to be reinforcing only if it increases or maintains the rate of responding.*

The gum-chewing incident in the Introduction provides a good example of a consequence (teacher's attention) of behavior (gum chewing) actually increasing the frequency of occurrence of the behavior. By our definition, the teacher's attention can be seen to have served the function of a reinforcing stimulus, despite the fact that the teacher intended it to be punitive.

NEGATIVE REINFORCEMENT

There is another set of situations that also has the effect of increasing or maintaining the strength or frequency of a response. Take the case of a high school student who is forced to go to a classroom against his will (which is not an atypical situation). Since he hates this class very much, he is continually searching for ways to get out of or avoid it. One day he disrupts the class by talking to other students and by passing notes back and forth; as a result, the teacher sends him out to stand in the hall. This situation is analogous to placing a rat in an experimental chamber whose metal floor can deliver an electric shock. When the shock is delivered, the rat will attempt to escape by trial and error. If he happens to press the bar that terminates the shock, the effect on subsequent trials is to *strengthen* the response that terminated the aversive (annoying) stimulus—namely, to strengthen the bar-press, since it removed the shock. In like manner, the consequence of removing the student from the classroom he hates has the effect of increasing the frequency of the disruptive responding that was responsible for his removal.

In both cases, student and rat, termination or avoidance of an annoying situation can be said to be reinforcing, since the effect of it was to increase or maintain the frequency of the behavior that removed it. This, then, constitutes a definition of **negative reinforcement:** *the removal or avoidance of an aversive stimulus as a consequence of the performance of a response.* Note that, as in positive reinforcement (which is the presentation of an attractive stimulus as a consequence of some response), the response rate must be increased or maintained in order to conclude that reinforcement did in fact occur.

As you can now see, contrary to popular opinion, *negative reinforcement is not a synonym for punishment*. Punishment is defined as the presentation of an annoying stimulus as a result of the performance of a response, and thus it is procedurally different from negative reinforcement. In addition, punishment has the opposite effect of negative reinforcement—punishment results in a decrease in the rate of the response that produced it. Our student would likely stop passing notes if, every time he did, he received a very strong electric shock through a grid in the chair to which he was strapped. (Though this would probably work, we do not recommend such treatment.)

EXTINCTION

If a reinforcing stimulus such as food to a hungry animal is withheld from an animal trained to press the bar for food, after many such trials the animal's bar-pressing response will decrease in frequency and may disappear entirely. This procedure of withholding reinforcement following a response is called *extinction,* and its effect is to decrease the rate of the behavior. Extinction of operants is therefore similar in procedure and effects to extinction of respondents.

OPERANTS AND RESPONDENTS COMPARED

As rules of thumb for distinguishing between respondent and operant conditioning, keep the following differences in mind. Operant behavior can be defined as behavior whose rate or strength is governed by its consequences. It is behavior that operates on the environment and is therefore emitted or voluntary. No preceding stimulus is necessary for an operant to occur, but the stimulus that follows (the consequence) determines whether the operant will occur again and at what rate or strength it will occur.

Classical conditioning, on the other hand, deals with reflexive responses called respondents. These respondents are originally elicited in an involuntary manner by a stimulus that precedes them (an unconditioned stimulus). By repeatedly presenting a neutral stimulus immediately before or simultaneously with the presentation of the unconditioned stimulus, the reflex can be brought under the control of the neutral stimulus (which is then called the conditioned stimulus). Thus the important stimuli are presented preceding, rather than following, the behavior, and no consequences are attached to the behavior.

As a final comparison of the two types of responses, consider some of the types of behaviors most often associated with operants and respondents. Included as operants are movements of all kinds, speech, studying, and writing. Classified as respondents are motor reflexes such as eye blinks, salivation, and the startle response, as well as a host of physiological responses often associated with emotional behavior, such as changes in heart rate, blood pressure, and hormone secretion.

CONDITIONING IN COMPLEX SITUATIONS

In practice, it may be difficult to classify a behavior (such as Albert's conditioned fear) as the result of classical or operant conditioning. This is especially true in complex learning situations, which occur in schools, that involve aspects of both classical and operant-conditioning procedures. For example, when a trainer uses pieces of candy to train a mentally deficient child in some personal skill and makes giving candy contingent on a small step forward in improvement of the child's skill level, he is using a technique based on operant-conditioning principles. At the same time, the association of the trainer as a dispenser of candy can induce a conditioned emotional response in the child. This association of trainer and candy can occur according to classical-conditioning principles, since the trainer (conditioned stimulus) presents the candy (unconditioned stimulus), which may produce an emotional response, such as happiness.

This kind of conditioned emotional response is particularly important in punishment procedures, which we will discuss later. For instance, a father's angry voice (conditioned stimulus) may come to signal a spanking (unconditioned stimulus), which elicits the response of crying or fear from the child.

While both kinds of conditioning are significant to success in develg effective child-training techniques, the main emphasis in this text is placed on operant conditioning. Operant-conditioning principles, when followed in the ways suggested in this book, not only provide the user with procedures for changing maladaptive behaviors but simultaneously create the supportive kind of environment necessary to conditioning positive, rather than negative, emotional respondents.

REINFORCEMENT EFFECTIVENESS

While it is true that the rate of a response can be increased or maintained by presenting a reinforcing stimulus after the emission of the response, various factors affect the efficiency with which this process occurs. Some of the more important factors that affect reinforcement efficiency are: (a) type of reinforcement, (b) quantity of reinforcement, (c) delay of reinforcement, (d) the reinforcement contingency, (e) the deprivation-satiation history of the organism, and (f) chance reinforcement effects.

TYPE OF REINFORCEMENT

Different individuals prefer different things, have different interests, and so on. This fact suggests that a stimulus providing an incentive for one individual may not be able to be used as a reinforcer for another individual. Teachers have long known that a high grade or gold star is an adequate reinforcer for some students in that it maintains the student's performance at a high level. Other students are not willing to work for a high grade—grades are just not reinforcing to them. In these cases, the teacher has to *find* stimuli that will maintain or increase the work responses of each individual student. Here is the point at which students' preferences can be used to great advantage, with the teacher using more preferred activities (such as allowing a basketball player who hates arithmetic free time to shoot baskets as a reward for a given number of correctly completed arithmetic problems). We will expand this discussion later.

QUANTITY OF REINFORCEMENT

Other things being equal, the greater the quantity of reinforcement, the greater the probability of the response being performed. This again is not surprising. Given a choice of shoveling snow for Mr. Jones, who pays $2, or Mr. Smith, who pays $1 for the same amount of work, anyone will choose to shovel for Mr. Jones. On the other hand, as the child grows older and/or inflation sets in, he is less likely to shovel snow for Mr. Jones, even for $2 an hour, because the quantity of reinforcement is not sufficient to maintain the response rate when other competing responses (such as playing guitar in a rock group) receive so much more social and monetary reinforcement.

Another way in which the quantity of a reinforcer affects the response rate goes under the name of stimulus **satiation.** If a stimulus is made available in excessive amounts, it can lose its reinforcing value. This becomes obvious when we sit down to a Thanksgiving Day dinner and gorge ourselves on turkey, then follow it up with several days of turkey sandwiches, salads, and omelets. Following this, most of us will avoid helping the neighbor paint his fence if the sole promised reward is a free turkey dinner.

In a similar manner, activities can be satiated. In his book *Summerhill,* A. S. Neill (1960) described the reaction of newcomers to his school: they avoided anything having to do with schoolwork for the first few weeks or, in extreme cases, even months. It seems that these students had been deprived of play and social interaction while being thoroughly satiated on schoolwork. Once a reasonable balance of response rates was again achieved, the Summerhill newcomers returned of their own choice to academic work.

DELAY OF REINFORCEMENT

It would be difficult to imagine teaching a new response to a rat or a pigeon if the food reinforcement were not delivered immediately after the response occurred. Once the response has been learned and practiced awhile, however, the reinforcement may be delayed for longer and longer periods (but there is probably always some optimal interval beyond which delays would not maintain the response).

There are many cases in which a salary is insufficiently reinforcing to maintain work behavior. George, for example, never worked a full week in his life on a salaried job. As soon as he finished a day or two at a job, he asked for his pay, left for the pool hall, and gambled away most of his money. No one could understand his job record. Finally he found a job at an agency that furnished 1-day laborers to companies for short jobs. He worked at this job for 6 years. George found the delay of the payment of his salary on a 1- or 2-week basis too much of a strain, whereas payment after each day's work was a much more effective personal system.

Children often require even more immediate reinforcement, at least in the beginning stages of learning a new response. The best rule in conditioning child behavior, therefore, is to make reinforcement as immediate as possible after the desired response occurs. The more reinforcement is delayed, the less effective it becomes.

REINFORCEMENT CONTINGENCIES

When reinforcement is made available to the individual following performance of one response but not following performance of another response, the relationship established between the behavior and delivery of reinforcement is called a **reinforcement contingency.** If a rat is given a pellet of food after every time it presses a bar but not after it pushes a button, a reinforcement contingency has been established. Reinforcement is dependent or contingent on the bar-press response.

Although there are some technical distinctions between reinforcement contingencies and rules, for our purposes, a reinforcement contingency can be considered a rule about which responses are necessary to bring rewards and which are not. As another example, consider the following rule that parents often state: when you finish your homework, you may watch television. This rule states the conditions under which television will be available as a reinforcement—namely, only after homework has been finished. The reinforcer, television, has been made contingent on the homework behavior.

What would happen if the parents allowed the child to watch television whether or not his homework was finished? The child would very likely not do his homework. The television would not be contingent on the homework behavior, and therefore the parents could not expect to increase the frequency of the child's homework behavior. Reinforcement would be noncontingent, and if the child does not have to perform a response to get a reward, why should he?

Reinforcement contingencies have probably been used and misused by grandmothers and in old wives' tales since time immemorial. (As Linus once said to Charlie Brown, "Some of those old wives were pretty sharp.") Few laymen have ever stated the idea more clearly, however, than Benjamin Franklin (reported by Skinner, 1969) when he counseled a Presbyterian chaplain. It seems that the enlisted men in the chaplain's outfit had been promised a gill of rum a day as an enlistment bonus. And while they were always on time for the serving of rum, few attended the prayers and services conducted by the chaplain. Franklin simply suggested that the rum be given out only immediately after prayers. The chaplain tried the idea with this result, in Franklin's words:

> Never were prayers more generally and more punctually attended; so that I thought this method preferable to the punishment inflicted by some military laws for non-attendance on divine service [p. 247].

The manner in which reinforcement is made available in relation to the organism's pattern of responding is critical to successful behavioral management. Response rates are increased when we learn that some reward is attached. Response rates are decreased when we expect some reward and it is not given. If reinforcement is not contingent on a response, a person will not work for it. If parents fail to be consistent in the way they respond to a child's behavior, they lose control over that behavior. As a side effect, the child can also become frightened or uneasy when his parents' responses to his behavior are inconsistent. He needs to learn to predict how a parent will respond when he does something. Strict adherence to contingency rules, therefore, is not only more effective in managing behavior from the standpoint of the parent but is also more desirable from the standpoint of the child.

CHANCE REINFORCEMENT AND SUPERSTITIOUS BEHAVIOR

As with respondent conditioning, it is not necessary that there be a logical or purposeful connection between behavior and reinforcement for operant conditioning to occur. Many superstitious behaviors persist in humans because of a random reinforcement. A professional baseball player's wife, for instance, wore the same article of clothing throughout a world series because her husband hit a home run the first day she wore it. Likewise, in the *Peanuts* comic strip, Linus' belief in the Great Pumpkin is maintained by unexplained movements he perceives in his sincere pumpkin patch. These random events serve as reinforcers for his expectation that the Great Pumpkin will appear and maintain his belief in the Great Pumpkin, despite the fact that he never receives any objective evidence (such as toys or candy) that the Great Pumpkin exists.

In complex school situations, a teacher may often be unaware that he does or says something to a student that may serve to reinforce the behavior the student was engaged in. In other words, the teacher's attention may randomly reinforce a behavior that was occurring. For example, intending to be warm and sincere, an attractive teacher may unknowingly reinforce a student's sexual advances. Such events, often leading to unpleasant confrontations later, demonstrate that the control chance reinforcement has over behavior is difficult to overestimate. The actual contingency—not the purpose of the reinforcement agent or teacher—is the important variable.

Guidelines for reinforcement contingencies. It is not enough, however, to state a reinforcement contingency when you wish to encourage one response instead of another. The following outline lists the main points to consider when you attempt to alter human behavior using a reinforcement contingency:

1. Choose a rule (contingency) that can be understood and followed by the student. (*Note*: There is no reason why a democratic method or the student himself should not decide what the rule should be. Rules do not have to be—and indeed will often be less effective when—imposed by an autocrat.)
2. Choose a rule that can be described clearly and objectively.
3. Choose a rule that can be enforced.
4. Make sure that the reinforcement is given consistently each time the correct response occurs.
5. Never present reinforcement before or without satisfactory completion of the task.
6. Ignore irrelevant behavior that is used by the student to get you to relax the contingency requirements (he is testing the limits of the rules).
7. Do not devise or enforce unnecessary or unreasonable rules.
8. Introduce and enforce rules one by one, rather than presenting several rules at once (especially with young children).

DEPRIVATION-SATIATION HISTORY

A rat will not press the bar for a reinforcing stimulus such as food or water unless he has been deprived of that reinforcer prior to the conditioning session. Any consequence of behavior is not necessarily effective in and of itself but depends on the deprivation-satiation history of the rat. Similarly, a teacher who plans to have students use free time to do homework as a reward for students who finish a classroom assignment early may find that this is not reinforcing to those students who just came from a study hall, but is to those students who had no free period during the day. The former students have a satiation history with regard to a particular potential reinforcing stimulus, while the latter have a deprivation history.

PRIMARY AND SECONDARY REINFORCEMENT

Some reinforcers have the power to strengthen behavior almost from the day one is born. This is because they satisfy a biological need; food is an example of such a reinforcer. Other examples of reinforcers that satisfy biological needs are water, sleep, and sexual stimulation. Reinforcers of this type do not need to be learned; they are reinforcing because of the biological nature of humans and animals. For this reason they are called **primary reinforcers.**

But, as is well known, behaviors can be strengthened by stimuli other than primary reinforcers, such as money, praise, or a smile. These stimuli are **conditioned** or **secondary reinforcers,** so called because they acquire reinforcing properties by being paired with primary reinforcers.

Money, for instance, is not reinforcing to a newborn baby, but it is not too many years later that money comes to be able to affect response rates. Let us consider how money may come to acquire reinforcing properties. A child in a store sees candy (the stimulus) and responds "Candy, please." The adult then provides the child with money, which he exchanges for candy (reinforcer).

Two aspects of this process should be noted carefully. First, the stimulus money became associated with the reinforcer candy by being paired with it. But second, the stimulus money not only accompanied the reinforcer but preceded it. For a neutral stimulus such as money to acquire reinforcer status, it must occur before the reinforcer. (Notice that, if the stimulus occurred after the reinforcer, the response would already have been reinforced and the neutral stimulus would be irrelevant to the process. Thus it could never come to reinforce the response.)

After many pairings of neutral stimulus and reinforcer in this manner, the previously neutral stimulus (money) acquires reinforcing properties, and people will respond in ways that will increase their chances of receiving money as a payoff. This, of course, is just another way of saying that money has acquired the defining properties of a reinforcing stimulus—it increases the rate of some kind of responding.

But what would happen if, all of a sudden, all the governments of the world decided that money would no longer be exchanged for goods or services? It would not be long before people stopped working for money. Money would have lost its secondary reinforcing qualities because it would no longer be connected with such primary reinforcers as food. The implication of this is that secondary reinforcers must be backed up by primary reinforcement, at least occasionally.

TYPES OF SECONDARY REINFORCERS

There are three classes of secondary reinforcers: social reinforcers, tokens, and activities. **Social reinforcers** include praise, social acceptance, smiles, and other human interactional stimuli. It is actually a moot question whether many of these social reinforcers are not actually primary reinforcing stimuli, and the question will not be resolved here. For convenience, they are included here under secondary reinforcers.

Tokens are a second class of secondary reinforcers, and they include physical objects or records that increase or maintain response rates. Examples are money, grades, and points.

The third type of secondary reinforcer has already been mentioned many times: **activities.** The principle governing use of activities as reinforcing stimuli (Premack's principle—Premack, 1959) is that, of two activities, the more preferred may be used to increase the rate of the less preferred. That is, an activity in which a person is interested, and therefore in which he spends a larger proportion of his time, can be used to reinforce responses in an activity in which the person is less interested and therefore spends less time. If a child likes to dance but does not like to read, dancing may be used to increase the amount of time the child spends reading, but not vice versa.

Of these secondary reinforcers, activities offer the greatest variety of potential reinforcing stimuli. The important point to keep in mind is that any one activity may or may not be an effective incentive for a given child. The teacher or parent who wants to find effective reinforcing stimuli, therefore, will take care to find out what the child's individual preferences are at any given moment. One efficient way of doing this, often forgotten, is to ask the student what would be an adequate incentive for him to do a certain task.

The practical applications of these principles of secondary reinforcers are many. The schools have traditionally used tokens, such as grades or stars, as secondary reinforcers. Unfortunately, the tokens are most often used noncontingently, in the sense that they are not given for the performance of a particular behavior but for the relative performance of one student in relation to the norm provided by the performance of other students. This type of competitive grading means that one student can succeed only at the expense of other students, which makes the reinforcer not contingent on each student's individual performance. In addition, teachers often give grades to punish a student for behaviors that are irrelevant to the objectives of a course. Because of this, course grades are usually noncontingent with regard to performance.

A better way to use tokens in the schools is like the professional football teams do. Many of these teams award stars (which are pasted on the player's helmet) to a defensive player who makes a certain number of unassisted tackles or interceptions. Each player who earns the stars receives them. In classrooms a similar use of tokens is applied with a mastery-learning approach, in which each student's grade is contingent on his own learning of the course objectives—a criterion-referenced, as opposed to a norm-referenced, grading system (see Chapter VII for further discussion of this issue).

Classroom uses of the Premack principle are also many and varied. Many elementary teachers schedule a free play period sometime during the day. Unfortunately, it is often scheduled rigidly to occur at a certain time each day for all students. This free period could be better used by allowing each student to select activities at natural breaks in the classwork, such as when a student has successfully completed a unit of work or has been task-oriented for some reasonable period of time.

Another use of the Premack principle can solve some of the problems of physical-education teachers in inner-city high schools. In many school systems, the curriculum calls for a unit of instruction on soccer, but the students would rather play basketball. Many teachers, especially student teachers, have found themselves confronted with a strike when they told the students that the next few weeks would be spent on soccer instead of basketball. In many cases, such problems have been solved or avoided simply by the establishment of a mutually agreeable contract based on the Premack principle—namely, a contract allowing students to play basketball toward the end of each period (or 1 or 2 days a week), contingent on their playing soccer the other times. Notice that this procedure is not only consistent with contingent reinforcement principles, but also with reasonable bargaining procedures of any kind in which mutual consent must be achieved.

THE EMOTIONAL EFFECTS OF REINFORCERS

Although it was mentioned earlier, it bears repeating that reinforcing stimuli and the people who hand them out often become conditioned stimuli (through respondent conditioning) for emotional responses. This process sometimes appears in cartoon satire, for example, when a secretary is saying "I can't imagine why I like Mr. Peterson. He's not handsome or rich, and he's not my type at all. But just the sight of him makes me feel good." And, of course, it turns out that Mr. Peterson is the company pay clerk.

The fact that previously neutral people and objects can be endowed with the power to elicit positive (or negative) feelings through mere association with a reinforcing (or punishing) situation is of immense practical importance. In classrooms, for example, it means that *you can never teach knowledge, skill, or "cognitive process" without at the same time connecting some emotion or feeling to the content, materials, or teacher.* The question is not whether to teach affect in the schools, but whether the affect will be positive or negative.

Consider a child who comes to school expecting to learn how to read but for some reason finds it more difficult to grasp the basics than do his classmates/competitors. If his teacher or his peers ridicule him, treat him as inferior (perhaps by placing him in the "dumb" reading group), or generally make his reading environment punishing, he is being conditioned to have negative feelings toward reading. Later on, this conditioning may show up in the labels teachers will assign to the child on his permanent record—labels such as "poorly motivated," "undisciplined," or "dyslexic." For this child there is almost no way in which you call learning to read a cognitive activity: his conditioned responses to reading (what we commonly call gut feelings) will interfere with serious cognitive activity.

The solution to this problem, as well as the way to prevent other such cases, is to make the consequences of reading very positive. In a classroom environment that is warm and rewarding, in which a child's attempts at reading are met with success, praise, and perhaps a preferred activity, a child can be conditioned to feel relaxed and comfortable with reading. Hence the importance of reinforcers is not only in their power to change the frequencies of observable behaviors (operant conditioning) but also in their capacity to transfer the feelings associated with them to neutral stimuli such as books, letters, or other reading symbols (respondent conditioning).

Notice that this is not a behaviorist plot to change the attitudes of students against their wills; this is the natural phenomenon of learning to like anything. For many of us, reading became a positive, preferred activity because, as young children, we saw our parents doing it and because, when we picked up books, our parents were likely to sit snuggled up with us for long periods of time. The comfort, warmth, and undivided attention they provided were sufficient to induce classically conditioned positive emotional responses to the act of reading.

A CLASSROOM EXAMPLE OF INCREASING RESPONSE RATES

Hall, Lund, and Jackson (1968) used the principles discussed in this unit to increase study behaviors in six elementary school children whose behavior was disruptive or dawdling. First, they defined the terminal behavior or final correct response that was desired. A *study response* was defined as orientation toward the object or person to be studied, such as the teacher or a book (looking at the teacher was a study response when the teacher was lecturing the class).

Next, a base rate of study responses was obtained. To do this, the observer sat in the rear of the classroom and recorded the rates of study of each of the children. Recordings were made on a recording sheet that divided each minute into 10-second intervals. The observer, by placing an S or an N on the recording sheet, simply recorded whether each student was engaging in study behavior or nonstudy behavior for more than half of each 10-second interval. This was done for 30 minutes a day at a time when the students were working at their seats. These observations were made 2 to 4 times a week for at least 2 weeks. The baseline data or base rates were obtained by calculating the percent of responses that were study responses.

Third, a stimulus was selected to reinforce study behaviors in these children. Attention from the teacher (such as the teacher's approaching the child, patting him on the shoulder, or saying "You are working very well") was selected as the reinforcing stimulus. The teacher rewarded the child with social reinforcement for performing a study response and ignored all nonstudy responses, making reinforcement contingent or dependent on a study response.

For one of the children, Robbie, the average base rate of study responses after seven observation sessions was 25% study behaviors, 75% nonstudy behaviors. The average percent of study behaviors over nine reinforcement sessions was 71%. In other words, the teacher's use of social reinforcement increased the rate of study responses from 25% to 71%.

Fourth, the teacher returned to her previous methods of responding to the children (which usually consisted of responding to nonstudy behaviors) to determine what effect withdrawing reinforcement would have on Robbie's study behaviors. Over the next five sessions, study responses dropped to an average of 50%.

Finally, to evaluate further the effects of contingent reinforcement of study behaviors, the teacher returned to praising study behaviors and ignoring nonstudy behaviors. Study responses again increased and stabilized at a 70% to 80% rate. Periodic follow-up sessions later in the school year revealed that this high study rate was continuing successfully.

Hall, Lund, and Jackson concluded that the use of teacher attention as a reinforcer contingent on study responses can be a quick and effective way to increase the rate of desirable study responses in a classroom.

A GENERAL PROGRAM FOR INCREASING RESPONSE RATES

As a review of the use of reinforcement to increase the rate of some behavior, here is a list of the steps involved.

1. Define the terminal or desired responses in clear behavioral terms so that there will be no confusion about whether a correct response did or did not occur.
2. Set up a favorable situation in which to condition the new responses. A favorable situation is one in which there are few distractions, incompatible responses are not being reinforced, and the correct response is likely to be performed.

3. Using a time-sampling technique (described earlier), obtain a base rate of the behaviors you are interested in. Recall that a base rate is a measure of the frequency of a response before attempts are made to change it. Express the baseline-response data as percentages or frequencies of responses occurring in a particular time period.
4. Select a stimulus to be used as a reinforcer. Recall that type, quantity, immediacy of delivery, and deprivation history must be considered in selecting a reinforcing agent.
5. Begin to change the rate of the response by delivering the reinforcer contingent on the performances of the response. That is, reinforce correct responses and ignore all others.
6. If the rate of the desired response does not increase after a reasonable length of time, re-evaluate your procedure to detect any errors you may be making or any other factors that may be interfering. For example, other people may be reinforcing undesirable responses. Also, re-evaluate the stimulus you have selected as a reinforcer. It may not be an effective reinforcer. In that case, select a different reinforcer. Then return to step 5 again.
7. If the rate of the desired response does show a reliable increase, prove that it is a result of the contingent application of reinforcement by withdrawing reinforcement for a few sessions. The response rate should drop.
8. Reintroduce contingent reinforcement. The frequency of the desired response should increase again to its previous high level.
9. Continue to record the response or periodically sample the response rate by the same time-sampling technique to ensure that the response is being maintained by the reinforcer.

CHAPTER THREE
SHAPING AND IMITATION

STUDY QUESTIONS

1. Define shaping.
2. What is meant by each of the following steps of shaping? Give an example.
   a. specify the terminal behavior.
   b. analyze the task for prerequisite behaviors.
   c. account for each individual's entering behavior.
   d. reinforce successively closer approximations.
3. Describe how shaping was used in the Kennedy Cottage program. Mention:
   a. the target behavior.
   b. the reinforcer.
   c. the levels of approximation to the desired behavior.
4. Define the following:
   a. imitation.
   b. observer.
   c. model.
   d. vicarious reinforcement.
5. What are some of the factors in which the effectiveness of vicarious reinforcement depends?
6. How are group dynamics related to the concepts of imitative behavior and vicarious reinforcement?
7. Describe how creative responding can be shaped.
8. After a food reward has been used to shape competent responding, will discontinuance of the food mean a decrease in the rate of the response? Explain, showing the relationship between attitudes and the development of new competencies.

THE TECHNIQUE OF SHAPING

So far this text has concentrated on the importance of observation and reinforcement of responses. When the correct response is emitted at the right time, reinforcement is given. If only conditioning were that simple!

Many new responses are never emitted spontaneously but must be developed from other, partially correct responses. In other words, correct responses must be *shaped* out of existing responses that may approximate to varying degrees the desired response. **Shaping** is the process of reinforcing closer and closer approximations of the desired behavior.

To shape a behavior not already in the student's repertoire, it is necessary first to specify in clear behavioral terms the desired terminal behavior—that is, the final end product you want. For example, suppose you want to teach a child to add two numbers. Your first step is to state the criterion behavior that you will accept as satisfactory evidence of adding ability. One such criterion might be that the child can add any two digits presented in any order orally or in writing with 90% accuracy.

The next stage in shaping any behavior is to analyze the task to determine what steps must be mastered and in what order before the terminal behavior can be attained. In the adding example, the student would probably be required to know how to count from 1 to 20 and be able to recognize those numerals when written as well as be able to write them.

Having defined the terminal response and specified the necessary prerequisite responses, you must now determine the student's entering behavior. In other words, you must find out what level of proficiency the student has already attained—what he is capable of. In this case, assume that the student is able to count from 1 to 20 and can recognize and write the numerals 0 to 9 but cannot write or recognize the written numbers 10 to 20.

The next step is to begin shaping the desired behavior by reinforcing each approximation to the desired performance. Reinforce the student for recognizing and writing the numerals 0 to 9 and for counting from 1 to 20.

Then raise the criterion and make reinforcement contingent on a closer approximation to the desired response. As each step is mastered, continue to reinforce successively closer approximations of the terminal behavior. When your student has convinced you that he is ready to recognize the numbers 10 through 20, present these numbers and reinforce each correct recognition. As this step is mastered, you can begin presenting objects in groups of two to begin to teach adding, using the student's mastery of counting (his entering behavior).

This procedure of reinforcing successively closer approximations is continued until the terminal behavior is attained—that is, until the student can add any two digits in the manner specified in the first step.

Described in this way, shaping sounds like a logical way of teaching anything, and, of course, it is. Successful teachers, parents, and animal trainers have been using it knowingly or unknowingly to train their students to perform complicated responses based on simple prerequisite behaviors. What is not so obvious is that for most organisms (humans included) and most tasks, successive reinforcement of closer and closer approximations is all that is needed for mastery of the terminal response. Punishment, threat, and ridicule are not necessary. The single additional requirement is the teacher's recognition that, if the student has not learned, the teacher has not taught. The responsibility for the student's not mastering the terminal behavior, in other words, is placed on the teacher's failure to arrange environmental conditions in such a way as to facilitate the student's correct performance. Therefore, if the student is not progressing at a pace the teacher feels is reasonable, it is up to the teacher to analyze the situation and find the reason for this failure of the program. The cause may be using an ineffective reinforcer, failing to begin shaping at the student's level of entering behavior, or moving too fast to higher levels of performance before previous levels have been mastered.

This last point of *moving on to new material before prerequisite materials have been mastered is probably the greatest single failing of educational systems.* If a student has not mastered a skill that is prerequisite to mastering a higher-order skill, it should not be surprising when he falters at the next level. Yet the lock-step process of much of education moves all students at the same rate through a curriculum, plotting each person's performance against that of his peers or against some national norm. Though such comparisons may be useful for some purposes, they are irrelevant to the individual's actual progress, which depends on his own mastery of each component of the skill being learned.

What would happen, for example, if an operant conditioner treated the individual differences in his pigeons in the same way that many schools treat individual differences in children? (See Gentile, 1972.) A 40-minute period would be established in which all pigeons would have to learn to peck a key in order to get food. In the next session they would have to turn a circle, then ring a bell, then peck the key to get food. As you can see, the behaviors required become more and more complex, and each successive step depends on mastery of the preceding one, much as in learning mathematics or reading.

Since each pigeon has a distinct genetic and experiential history (as does each human), some pigeons will learn the first task in only a few minutes, while others will require much longer than the allotted 40 minutes. This, of course, gives those who already knew how to peck the disc to earn food a significant advantage over those to whom the experimental chamber is a totally new experience. (We might even find a difference in tested IQ in favor of those pigeons who had previous experiences in apparatus related to the IQ-testing procedures.) The result would be that the pigeons that had mastered the first step would find it easier to learn steps 2 and 3, while those that had not mastered step 1 would fall further and further behind as we required closer and closer approximations of the desired terminal behavior.

The supreme irony of this example is that the schools face this problem each day and draw the conclusion that it is the child himself, his parents, or his sociocultural environment that is responsible for his "learning disability." The genetic endowment, parental rearing practices, and sociocultural environment do affect the child's learning rate, entering behavior, and motivation for learning, just as they affect these aspects of the pigeon's behavior. But to use genetics, rearing, and environment as the reasons for the child's (or pigeon's) failure to learn is, from an operant-conditioning point of view, unforgivable. Bloom (1968) estimates that fewer than 5% of individuals already in school cannot learn what the schools have to teach. So any failure to learn is probably due to a failure on the part of the teacher or administrator responsible for the student's environment. As in our example of the pigeons, failure at the first level would probably have been due to the instructor's failure to provide sufficient time, incentive, or both; failure at succeeding levels would probably have been due to those reasons as well as to the instructor's failure to begin at the entering level of the student (if he hadn't mastered task 1, why go on to task 2?).

There may be good administrative reasons for grouping children and moving them at the same general pace from one successive approximation to the next, but there are few if any reasons based on knowledge of the learning process. Each student must be allowed and encouraged to master each level of whatever objectives are established. If, for administrative convenience, this is not done, then conditions are not established for optimal learning, and blame for failure should be placed on the administrative procedures used. It all boils down to the basic idea that, if the student has not learned, the teacher (or administrator or both) has failed.

A CLASSROOM EXAMPLE: SHAPING STUDY BEHAVIORS

In special-education programs or in psychiatric institutions it is usually easy to see the usefulness of shaping and related techniques for increasing the rates of responses. Shaping, however, does not have to be limited to persons with serious mental disabilities. It has been used very successfully with persons of normal intelligence levels, as in the Kennedy Cottage program at Washington, D.C.'s Junior Village (Frazier, 1969), a residence home for children from preschool to high school ages, many of whom are orphans or have been in trouble with the law.

In the Kennedy Cottage program at Junior Village, an individual tutoring program was developed for cottage residents. For these children, who showed a wide variety of deviant behaviors (including physical assaults on others), one of the most significant adjustment problems was a lack of school attendance. Individual levels of academic skills varied from total illiteracy to performance at grade level. Daily attendance in the Washington, D. C., schools that they went to averaged about 50% prior to implementation of the tutoring program. One full-time teacher was employed for tutoring, with some short-term support by another teacher. The program manager worked closely with these teachers, and a system was established to build up appropriate study behaviors in the children.

The basic source of reinforcement was a system of earning and spending points. Children earned points (as the reinforcing stimulus) through engaging in a variety of activities considered important in building up personal, social, and academic skills. A cottage store was provided as one source of point-spending, and many other preferred activities were made available to the children who earned enough points to participate in them.

Early in the program it was decided to make effective studying behavior in the classroom the activity that would receive the highest number of points. Consequently, more points were made potentially available for school performance than for any other activity.

The shaping system operated in the following manner: the first problem was to get children to come to the classroom on their own. To attain this goal, the teachers gave the children 3 points each for reporting to class on time and staying for the entire class period. The next goal was to obtain satisfactory participation in studying behavior and responsiveness to teacher request. To reach this goal, the teacher had the option of dispensing 0 to 5 points for class response and participation. The points that could be obtained for simple attendance were not removed; instead, any points from the new source of earnings were added to the points that could be obtained for simple attendance.

The next step in shaping studying behaviors was to add a reinforcement contingency concerning test taking. Children were given from 0 to 5 points by the teacher, depending on their performance on tests.

The next step of the shaping procedure was to make 0 to 4 points available to the child for completing homework assignments satisfactorily. Again, this new source of points was simply added to the already established point-earning sources.

The final step of the academic program consisted of establishing a "bonus" system. The child was given additional bonus points whenever his total point earnings for academic behaviors exceeded the previous week's earnings. If a child earned 50 points one week in the tutoring program and 60 points the next week, he was given 10 additional bonus points. Thus a contingency was introduced to stimulate improvements in academic performance as time progressed.

Studying behavior was therefore broken down into the following components:

1. Coming to class on time and staying.
2. Participating in studying behavior and responding to the teacher.
3. Performing well on tests.
4. Completing homework.
5. Improving in performance as time progressed.

The results of this systematic approach to building up studying behaviors were dramatic. School attendance increased from the original baseline level of around 50% to an average of 86% after only a few months. More importantly, the students' behavior in class changed remarkably, from essentially unproductive use of time to highly relevant and effective study and greatly improved cooperation with the teacher.

The Kennedy Cottage tutoring program can be considered consistent with the rules of behavioral shaping. However, one important change was introduced. Instead of being required to perform successively better and better to obtain reinforcements, a child could always obtain reinforcement for each of the component behaviors. When a child became capable of more than just coming to class, he still was permitted to earn the points for coming to class. This departure from the traditional technique was quite effective for this shaping program, but such a departure is not a necessary addition to make such a program work effectively.

IMITATIVE BEHAVIOR AND VICARIOUS REINFORCEMENT

In "Social Learning through Imitation," Bandura (1963) provides the following description of the use of shaping procedures to teach driving a car. The instructor, who has filled his pockets with an assortment of gum, candy, and cigarettes, waits for the student to move toward the car and then hands him a piece of candy. After more seemingly random activity, the student makes another step toward the car and is promptly reinforced with a cigarette. After about an hour of patience and reinforcement of successively closer approximations, the instructor succeeds in shaping the student so that he touches the car door handle. Finally, he opens the car door and receives a stick of gum, sits in the front seat and is rewarded with more candy, and so on.

The point of this anecdote is that, while shaping is an effective means of strengthening response patterns, it is very inefficient when compared with imitation, the most frequently used method of learning. Nevertheless, imitative behavior appears to follow the same principles of stimulus control as other behaviors.

IMITATION: OBSERVERS AND MODELS

Imitative behavior is defined as the responses that are learned by an **observer** as a result of witnessing the behavior of some other person, called a **model.** A response class of "imitative behavior" can be defined and used regardless of the nature of the specific individual acts that constitute imitative responding. With this response class, the goal is to teach the observer to imitate what the model is doing. After the child has learned to imitate consistently, the instructor can concern himself with the details of training the child when the individual acts should be emitted.

Baer, Peterson, and Sherman (1967) have developed a technique for developing imitative behavior that is especially useful for young or retarded children. The first step involves shaping procedures. The trainer performs some response and then says "Do this." He may repeat this initial routine a number of times. After this step, the trainer may repeat the demonstration and then give the individual assistance by moving, pushing, or pulling him through performance of the correct response. This completion of the response, with help, is immediately reinforced. After several successful trials with assistance, the trainer begins to fade his assistance until the child is performing the response independently. Reinforcement is given each time the act is completed, immediately following its completion.

As the number of successfully imitated responses increases, it is less and less necessary to guide the person through the physical operation involved in the act, and the verbal statement "Do this" becomes much more effective in directing behavior. Later in the training, many responses can be executed perfectly after the first routine is completed (trainer performs the response and says "Do this").

Using this technique to induce vocal responding was more difficult. One way that worked to induce an initial response consisted of beginning with imitation of blowing out a match. This was shaped into more vigorous blowing, which included a loud "P" sound. The "P" was expanded into "pah" and then into a number of different vocalizations, all as reliable imitations.

One other feature of this match-blowing procedure was the eventual use of new models to induce imitative behavior. This procedure was used to ensure that responses made to one model would also be made to another model. This generalization of responses to new trainers was readily accomplished.

VICARIOUS REINFORCEMENT

Much of current advertising is based on the concept of vicarious reinforcement. When a television actor is observed obtaining some reward for using a manufacturer's product, the home viewer may be more likely to use the product himself. The commercial showing some relationship between using the product and subsequently getting a reward presumably has a vicarious effect on the viewer, almost as if he himself had received the reward. This imagined-reinforcement effect is a very important one, as the success of advertising programs on sales rates indicates.

Vicarious reinforcement is said to have occurred when the rate of an observer's response is increased or maintained as a result of seeing a model reinforced for making the same response. The observer is said to have imitated the behavior of the model. The consequences of the model's behavior appear to exert a similar influence on the observer's behavior. In other words, reinforcement of a model's response increases the rate of that response by the observer; nonreinforcement of the model's response (extinction) decreases the rate of the observer's response (although present evidence is not so definite with regard to vicarious-extinction effects). The effects of vicarious reinforcement, then, seem to parallel the effects of direct reinforcement.

Effects of vicarious reinforcement. Bandura and Walters (1963, p. 179) reported an interesting experiment on some of the effects of vicarious reinforcement on the imitative responses of children. The children participated in a bowling game in which the scores, which could range from 5 to 30, were controlled by the experimenter. In one condition, the model could be observed rewarding himself for obtaining high scores (20 or above) by taking a handful of candy, which was available for that purpose, and praising himself for making such a high score. In another experimental condition, the model rewarded himself for obtaining lower scores (10 or above) by making the same kind of self-approval or disapproval statements as the other model.

After observing their respective models, the children were permitted to bowl some games and to reward themselves. It was found that the children tended to reward themselves in the same way as the models they had observed. They tended to set the same minimum standards for candy reward, and they also imitated the same kinds of self-approving comments as their models.

Not only are self-approving comments adopted by individuals, but other factors that are often considered to be important for self-esteem can also be influenced through vicarious reinforcement. Warner and Hansen (1970) demonstrated, for example, that the amount of alienation and powerlessness high school students feel in regard to school and society can be shaped by exposure to role models. They established several group-counseling sessions for students who expressed attitudes of high alienation, such as lack of control over their destiny and lack of acceptance by their peers. Counseling sessions for one of these groups included a male and a female model. The models were also students from the same school, but they did not score high on the alienation scale and were highly rated by students and teachers in social acceptance and academic performance. The models were not aware of their role in the counseling session. In discussions of how the students could deal with their perceived powerlessness and isolation, however, these models were verbally reinforced by the counselor each time they made a statement that suggested positive attitudes or procedures to eliminate this alienation. Students in this group subsequently showed greater shifts in attitudes in the positive direction than did students in groups in which positive attitudes were not reinforced.

In another study, this one with elementary school children, Hansen, Niland, and Zani (1969) found that the students who were rated by their peers to be of low sociometric status showed the greatest gains in social acceptance after counseling sessions in which models were reinforced. In this study, vicarious-reinforcement effects were even more pronounced than direct-reinforcement effects, both of which were more effective than no counseling at all.

These studies show that the consequences of a model's behavior have a great effect not only on the model but on the observer. More importantly, this vicarious-reinforcement effect is not limited to the "cognitive domain" of skill or concept acquisition but apparently extends to the "affective domain" of values and attitudes as well. This is not a particularly surprising finding, but it is one that parents and educators have not used to their advantage nearly enough.

The Suzuki method (Pronko, 1969; Rosen, 1971) of teaching stringed instruments to very young children is one of the few methods incorporating vicarious-reinforcement ideas. With this method, a parent learns to hold the bow properly while the children sit and watch. The result of this is that the children wait eagerly for their chance to receive the attention the parent is receiving, simultaneously learning some of the skills being taught. The main effect of this procedure is that the child's motivation to learn the instrument increases; in addition, the parent learns patience with regard to the child's performance—an important benefit, since the children often outshine their parents within a few months.

Other factors: Side effects and group dynamics. Vicarious reinforcement can be a particularly useful concept in working with groups of children, as in token-economy systems or schools. If students can observe others (models) earning reinforcement for some desirable act, their rates of responding in the same way may be increased. The effectiveness of vicarious reinforcement, however, depends on such factors as the models' age, sex, dress, and other characteristics. These factors must be taken into account in order for vicarious reinforcement to be most effective.

There may be some unexpected side effects of vicarious reinforcement. For example, observers may learn not only the desired response class but also other unwanted behaviors. One common example of this is that we often begin to dress like those we admire. In addition, if the model is punished for some kind of responding, the observers may perform significantly fewer imitative responses.

Because vicarious reinforcement usually has a weaker effect than direct reinforcement in changing response rates, and because of some of the side effects just discussed, vicarious reinforcement alone is sometimes not appropriate to use for reinforcing imitative behavior. In these cases, reinforcement of the model's act must be followed by reinforcement of the student's own performance of the act. This procedure, of course, is the one recommended when direct reinforcement of the observer's correct response is possible.

It should be pointed out that much we label "group dynamics" refers to imitation and modeling behaviors. In any group, peer imitation becomes an important behavior of the individual and of the group as a whole. Consequently, in the classroom situation, the teacher must remain alert to the possibility that undesirable behaviors will arise and be maintained by imitation processes.

Cognizance of these group dynamics can often help the teacher solve and prevent behavior problems by using the group pecking order to his own advantage. For example, if a student who has the respect of the others can be seen being reinforced for desirable behaviors, the effect may be not only to increase the rate of the desirable behavior of this student but also to help shape the behavior of the observers. On the other hand, praising a student as a model of desirable behavior if he is not respected by other students may have an effect opposite to that intended. Thus the teacher must plan his reinforcement carefully and must, above all, know his students. Group processes are always complex because of the subtle interactions of vicarious- and direct-reinforcement processes among the various combinations of teacher-student groups and subgroups and individual students.

Sensitivity-training and encounter groups use behavior principles to emphasize *maintaining* the participation of the members of the groups. The "sensitive" trainer or group member is one who learns to watch the behaviors (verbal and nonverbal) of others in the group for signs of boredom, interest, and other feelings and moods. When a particular group member seems to be excluded, he can then be "reached" by some appropriate encouragement from the others. Indeed, many of the games and simulations used in training sessions are designed to demonstrate the effects of the group environment on the feelings (inclusion, exclusion, comfort, discomfort, and so on) and participation of the individual members.

Though there is still much to be learned in the area of group behavior, there is much to be gained by knowing your students well enough to be able to allow the natural group processes to be your allies in the classroom. One way to take advantage of group processes is to encourage students who have mastered certain material to help other students learn it. Many successful teachers do this now on an informal basis, arranging for first-grade students who can read to go to the kindergarten classes to read to those students. This serves the dual purpose of providing a peer model for the kindergarten students as well as allowing the model himself to be reinforced for his competence in reading. One ninth-grade earth-science class in the Nichols School in Buffalo (Price, 1970) became interested in ecology and decided it was an important enough topic to develop a curriculum to teach to fifth-graders. They were being reinforced by their teacher for this venture, and the end result would be their helping to teach fifth-graders.

One system was devised to formalize such help in a college course in principles of behavior (Johnston & Pennypacker, 1971). In this course, student assistants were selected from among the more successful students in the previous semester's course. They were enrolled in an individual work course for which they earned a grade. They earned a grade in the course for being personally responsible for the learning, including tutoring and testing, of several students in the behavior-principles course. Since the assistants' grades were primarily (though not entirely) contingent on the performance of their students, the assistants would track down a student who missed appointments, and so on. The course principles were learned quite efficiently by this technique. Moreover, the students in the behavior-principles course found the procedure quite valuable, and as many as half the class volunteered to be assistants in the next semester.

The benefits of a system like this are tremendous. The students being exposed to the curriculum for the first time do indeed learn the material, and their personal tutors learn it better because of the review. In addition, learning becomes a personal process, with each student having a chance to discuss the material, receive motivation, and so on from a peer. Such procedures could easily be adapted to public school situations, especially by capitalizing on the abilities and social concern of high school students to help younger students.

SHAPING, ATTITUDES, AND CREATIVITY

Just as there is a class of responses called "imitative behaviors" that can be shaped and maintained by reinforcement, there is a class of "creative behaviors" that can also be shaped. It is always difficult for educators to agree about what is meant by "creativity," especially when used by teachers in such phrases as "we are trying to encourage creativity." Nevertheless, if we assume that such a statement means that the individual can produce solutions to problems that are novel to him, then it is not too difficult to define a creative response for any given situation. By this definition, shaping creativity is no different from shaping anything else, since the whole concept of shaping refers to increasing the rate of a behavior that was never performed before by that individual.

One of the most influential writers on the topic of teaching creativity is Torrance (1970), who provides explicit procedures for what he calls "encouraging creativity in the classroom." Although he does not discuss it in these terms, his procedures reduce to the basic principle of shaping: encourage creative responses by establishing a situation in which such responding is likely (with appropriate materials, the freedom to try new things without threat of grading, and so on), and then give attention and praise to the creative efforts that are made. Torrance provides interesting materials and examples for what might be called an elementary curriculum for teaching creativity, and he finds that students do indeed show an increased frequency of creative responding.

This conception of encouraging children's creativity is not very different from the way animal trainers encourage creativity. Pryor (1969), for example, described the procedures used to shape a porpoise to perform novel tricks. The trainer first cataloged the movements the animal made and plotted their frequencies. This provided a base rate of the animal's behavior. Then at feeding time she watched the porpoise carefully but did not reinforce it with fish after any normal (high-frequency) behavior. Instead, the reinforcement was contingent on low-frequency or novel behavior. As each low-frequency or unique behavior was reinforced, it occurred at a higher frequency (as we would expect); then the criterion was raised so that the porpoise had to perform a different or more difficult new behavior. In a few weeks the porpoise was performing many novel and in some cases unique responses. The trainer still had to bring each command under some stimulus control so that the porpoise would know when to perform each trick, but this is a discrimination-learning problem. What is important for our present discussion is that the trainer was able to piece together a show of tricks invented by the porpoise, not the trainer. In fact, it is difficult to imagine how the trainer could establish objectives ahead of time for the behaviors the porpoise was capable of performing without first seeing them performed. These unique behaviors were available, but their appearance had to be encouraged by the technique of reinforcing infrequent responses.

ATTITUDES AND VALUES

We have seen how important shaping and imitation are in the development of such diverse activities as learning addition, attending school, gaining self-approval, and becoming socially acceptable—activities that cover both the so-called cognitive and affective domains of human behavior. Despite this wide range of applicability, the claim is often made that, if a person is reinforced with food, money, or praise, he will become hedonistic or materialistic and never enjoy learning for its own sake.

There are many ways to respond to this objection. First, there are many activities that all of us do only because there is a tangible payoff. Very few teachers, for example, would find their jobs sufficiently intrinsically motivating to teach for a year if the school board could not pay them. Even worse, to decry the use of incentives but then to use grades, punishment, and legal means to coerce students into going to school and doing the work whether they want to or not is hypocritical, to say the least.

Second, it is simply not the case that extrinsic reinforcement precludes the possibility of enjoying an activity for its own sake. Very few skills or conceptual abilities are intrinsically motivating to someone in the beginning stages of learning. To a child who cannot balance his bicycle and keeps falling off, there is nothing intrinsically motivating about riding. At this stage in his learning, he needs the encouragement and praise of adults as well as the vicarious reinforcement of observing his peers (as models) having fun riding their bikes. It is only after he gains sufficient skill in balancing to propel himself without fear of injury that riding can become rewarding for its own sake. Previous to that, the child spends a relatively small proportion of his time riding his bicycle; following attainment of the minimum necessary skill, the rate of bicycle riding increases markedly. Even though the behavior had to be maintained with social reinforcement in the early stages of learning, reinforcement is no longer necessary to maintain the response at a high rate once the behavior is learned.

Many parents use some variant of a penny game to motivate their children to learn the alphabet and phonetics preparatory to learning to read: for each letter (or more than one) the child correctly identifies, he receives a penny or a piece of candy. Such techniques are quite useful to motivate a child to attend to the symbols long enough to learn them, and the game can be fun, although the fun for the child is usually the payoff. Once the child learns to read, however, it is no longer necessary to reinforce his attending to books with pennies or candy, because reading itself can be fun.

The moral of these stories is that, as skills are developed, attitudes and values associated with the skills change in a positive direction. Bicycle riding is not a preferred activity until the children acquire the skill to ride proficiently; reading is similarly nonpreferred until the children can read. At that point the skill becomes a preferred activity; the children who previously would read or mount the bicycle only for the reward or praise they received from adults are now motivated for the pleasure of the activity itself. Many similar examples could be given, such as learning to write, speak a foreign language, or play a musical instrument; children (or adults) who are initially motivated to do something by some immediate and tangible payoff find that activity later to be very preferred—that is, the base rate of that behavior increases once mastery of the skill is obtained.

Our third argument for the use of reinforcement is that most reinforcement programs, including the principles presented in this book, encourage shaping the person to a state of intrinsic motivation by reducing the frequency of reinforcement following performance of the behavior. In other words, reinforcement provided continuously in the early stages of learning is provided only intermittently in the later stages. Intermittent reinforcement is one topic in the next chapter.

In addition, as progress in the skill develops, less emphasis should be placed on tangible reinforcers such as food and money, while more emphasis should be given to social reinforcers such as praise and attention. The individual will find that he has changed as a person, since he now has a new ability, and people will respond to him differently as a result. Thus the behavior will be maintained, and his image of himself will change accordingly. As Freidenberg (1959) puts it, a person's self-esteem is tied directly to his competencies: a person knows who he is by what he can do.

CHAPTER FOUR
SCHEDULES OF REINFORCEMENT

STUDY QUESTIONS

1. Define the following:
   a. continuous reinforcement.
   b. intermittent or partial reinforcement.
   c. schedule of reinforcement.
2. What is the difference between a ratio and an interval schedule?
3. Define and give an example of each of the following:
   a. fixed-ratio schedule.
   b. variable-ratio schedule.
   c. fixed-interval schedule.
   d. variable-interval schedule.
4. Compare the response rates of the following types of schedules:
   a. fixed- and variable-ratio schedules.
   b. fixed- and variable-interval schedules.
   c. fixed-interval and fixed-ratio schedules.
5. Why are intermittent-reinforcement schedules more resistant to extinction than continuous schedules are?
6. What is the best kind of schedule to use:
   a. to train a new response?
   b. to maintain a response rate?
7. How can a response established on a continuous schedule be shifted to an intermittent schedule?
8. How can schedules of reinforcement help solve such problems as short attention spans in students or teacher/student ratios?

TYPES OF REINFORCEMENT SCHEDULES

CONTINUOUS AND INTERMITTENT REINFORCEMENT

When some kind of response is reinforced every occasion on which it occurs, **continuous reinforcement** is being used. Reinforcing a new response on every occasion it is emitted is the quickest way to increase its frequency. Sometimes reinforcement is given on some but not all of the times the response occurs. In such cases, **partial** or **intermittent reinforcement** is being used. Intermittent reinforcement can be an effective way to maintain some new response once it has been initially established through continuous reinforcement. There are various ways in which intermittent reinforcement can be given, ways called *schedules of reinforcement.*

A schedule of reinforcement is a plan or description of the contingency dictating when or how often a response is reinforced. The two most commonly used types of reinforcement schedules are ratio and interval schedules. With a **ratio schedule,** reinforcement is provided only after some given number of *responses* has been emitted. With **interval schedules,** reinforcement is given only after some period of *time* has elapsed since the previous reinforcement. A ratio schedule is based on counting the number of responses, while an interval schedule is based on counting time intervals between reinforcements.

Ratio schedules. Under ratio schedules, reinforcement is made contingent on the number of responses performed, without regard to the amount of time taken to perform the response. There are two major types of ratio schedules: the **fixed-ratio schedule** and the **variable-ratio schedule.** With a fixed-ratio schedule, the number of responses required to obtain reinforcement is always the same. For example, reinforcement may be given after every 5 responses. This would be called a fixed-ratio:5 (FR:5) schedule. An FR:10 schedule would provide reinforcement after every 10 responses. The number of responses necessary for reinforcement is not varied under a fixed-ratio schedule.

With the variable-ratio schedule, the subject still has to perform some number of responses to obtain a single reinforcement. However, the exact number of responses required is varied, so that the subject never knows the exact number required for reinforcement. Variable-ratio schedules are described in terms of the average number of responses required for reinforcement. A variable-ratio:20 (VR:20) would dispense reinforcement after 20 responses *on the average.* The exact number of responses might vary from one reinforcement after every 5 responses to one reinforcement after every 40 responses, but the number of responses necessary to receive a reinforcement would average 20 over some sequence. Such a sequence of responses necessary for a reinforcement might be the following: 18, 27, 12, 23, 10, 20, 30.

Interval schedules. With an interval schedule, reinforcement is made to depend on the amount of time that has passed since the last opportunity for reinforcement; that is, *after the prescribed time interval, the next correct response will be reinforced.*

The two basic types of interval schedules are called **fixed interval** and **variable interval.** A fixed-interval schedule is based on some constant unit of time between successive reinforcements. For example, a fixed-interval:1 (FI:1) schedule would dispense reinforcement after the first correct response occurring 1 minute or more following previous reinforcement. A FI:10 schedule would provide reinforcement for the first correct response following a 10-minute interval since the last reinforcement.

A variable-interval schedule provides reinforcement intermittently following the first correct response after a specified time has elapsed. The subject can never anticipate when the next reinforcement is due. Variable-interval schedules are described in terms of the *average* interval programmed between successive reinforcements. For example a variable-interval:5 (VI:5) schedule would be one in which a reinforcement would be made available for a correct response after every 5 minutes on the average. The exact spacing of reinforcements would sometimes be less and sometimes be more, as in the following sequence: the first correct response after 2 minutes, 7 minutes, 10 minutes, 1 minute.

RESPONSE RATES AND THE VARIOUS SCHEDULES

Each of these different reinforcement schedules induces different patterns of responding. When responding has stabilized on any given schedule, it always takes a highly consistent form, which can be easily identified and distinguished from response patterns on other schedules of reinforcement.

Because ratio schedules reward the number of responses, persons or animals working under the control of ratio schedules respond at a high and fairly steady rate. A rat on a fixed-ratio:50 schedule soon learns that he must press the bar 50 times before he earns a reinforcing pellet of food. His rate of responding is therefore quite high—that is, he usually emits all 50 responses very quickly and in a highly rhythmic form. Similar behavior is emitted by factory workers or salesmen on a piece rate.

On a variable-ratio schedule, the response rate is also very high but slightly more steady. This is because the subject can never determine exactly when reinforcement will be delivered. An example of a variable-ratio schedule maintaining a high and consistent response rate is that of a gambler playing a slot machine. He does not know how many coins he must put in the machine before his next reinforcement. It is always possible that the next response will be reinforced. Therefore he responds at a high, rhythmic rate, with very little pausing, except to pick up the coins delivered by the machine.

Because interval schedules do not depend on the number of responses given, but only on the amount of time that has passed, a rat will emit *many fewer responses in a given time under an interval schedule than under a ratio schedule.* On a fixed-interval: 10 schedule, for example, an experienced rat would probably not respond at all for the first 5 minutes following reinforcement. Then his response rate will slowly increase as the end of the 10-minute interval approaches, because after 10 minutes his next response gets reinforced.

This is similar to the behavior of an individual who is waiting for a bus. If he knows a bus comes every 10 minutes, his looking-down-the-street response will become more frequent the closer it comes to the end of the 10-minute interval. If a bus comes by but is full, he will stop looking for a while, then start looking more and more frequently when the next bus is due. Both the rat and the man are responding under fixed-interval schedules.

Under variable-interval schedules, the rate of response is also lower than under ratio schedules. However, the rate of response is more consistent under a variable-interval schedule than under a fixed-interval schedule. This is because the individual never knows exactly when his next response will be reinforced. Contrast the man watching for a bus with the man watching for a taxi. Since taxis come at variable intervals (not on the relatively fixed-interval schedules of buses), the man must keep looking for the taxi, but not necessarily at a high rate, since he cannot predict exactly when a taxi will pass by.

THE WORK HABITS OF CONGRESS: THE EFFECTS OF A FIXED-INTERVAL SCHEDULE

It is a striking phenomenon that the plotted behavior of various species on the same reinforcement schedule is so similar. We have already noted the characteristic high and steady rates of behavior evidenced both by pigeons and by human slot-machine players on ratio schedules—both peck away at a high rate, pausing only to collect their rewards or to collapse from fatigue.

Weisberg and Waldrop (1972) recently showed that the United States Congress is controlled by a relatively pure case of a fixed-interval schedule. In this case the powerful reinforcer of vacation time (among others) is contingent on appropriate work behavior, which for Congress is acting on bills. But it is not the number of bills passed that determines when vacation starts; rather, it is the time of year. By tradition, congressional sessions begin and end within a relatively consistent time span. Thus the defining characteristics of a fixed-interval:9 months' schedule are present—namely, a fixed month of adjournment and recess contingent on appropriate work (defined as deliberating, filibustering, and referring to committees, in addition to passing bills).

When Weisberg and Waldrop plotted the number of bills passed by eight Congresses from 1947 to 1968, they found in each case the characteristic fixed-interval response rate. In each of the two sessions of every Congress, relatively few bills are passed during the first 3 or 4 months after the Congress is called into session, followed by an increasing acceleration in the number of bills passed up until the day of adjournment.

RESISTANCE TO EXTINCTION

We are all accustomed to receiving one reinforcement for every coin we place in a candy machine. In other words, our response of depositing a coin is reinforced on a continuous schedule. However, what happens to the rate of response if we drop in a coin and do not receive the candy reinforcement? Our rate of response will drop off quickly. In fact, we are likely not to drop any more coins in the candy machine. This nonreinforcement of a previously reinforced response is called extinction. When a previously continuously reinforced response is extinguished, the response rate falls off very rapidly.

Compare this with the gambler playing the slot machine. He is on a partial-reinforcement schedule; that is, he must emit many responses in order to receive reinforcement. What happens to the rate of response if he drops in a coin and does not get a payoff? The answer is that the response rate will probably not be affected. He will continue to respond at a high rate because he will not know that reinforcement is being withheld—that extinction procedures are being used. He is used to making many responses that are not reinforced, and therefore his response is more **resistant to extinction.** An intermittent-reinforcement schedule produces response patterns that take a long time to be extinguished.

SHAPING RESPONDING TO INTERMITTENT SCHEDULES

Because intermittent-reinforcement schedules produce response rates that are quite stable and resistant to extinction, these schedules are used to *maintain* responses already learned. However, in training a new response, intermittent reinforcement is much less effective than continuous reinforcement. A reinforcement for each correct response or successive approximation helps the individual to learn the behavior much faster than if some of his responses are not reinforced. Thus a new response should be trained on a continuous-reinforcement schedule when possible.

After a behavior has been developed by reinforcing every correct response, the trainer can begin to change the schedule a little at a time. That is, he might reinforce every other response one day, then every third response the next day, and so on, slowly increasing the ratio of number of responses made to each reinforcement. By this procedure, responding on a ratio schedule can be produced.

If the trainer slowly increased the amount of time before the next response were reinforced, he could develop responding on an interval schedule. Thus he might reinforce the first response that occurred after 10 seconds, then 15 seconds, then 20 seconds, and so on.

In practical situations it is often useful to know the characteristic response rates produced by the different schedules. For example, a teacher might use a ratio schedule to maintain a high rate of correct answers on arithmetic tests or spelling words. She could reinforce the child for some fixed or variable number of correct answers, which should have the effect of increasing the number completed.

Interval schedules can also be used to great advantage in teaching situations. A teacher would have difficulty counting the number of study responses in order to reinforce individual students on a ratio schedule. However, he could arrange to keep track of periods of time in which the students have been emitting study responses and reinforce those responses on a variable-interval schedule. Thus, after a student has worked correctly for a short while, the teacher can tell him he is doing a good job. At first these reinforcements may need to be given every few minutes to establish the behaviors, but later the reinforcers will adequately maintain the responses after increasingly longer intervals.

TWO PRACTICAL PROBLEMS

ATTENTION SPANS

A common problem for teachers, especially for teachers of special-education classes, is the child who is known for having a short attention span. Often what is called a short attention span is considered one symptom of a more serious syndrome of difficulties, such as in the case of children diagnosed as hyperactive. Ignoring the problem of diagnosing or clinically labeling a child, we wish to make the point that one of the major problems is simply that the child, in someone's opinion, does not attend long enough to the presented task. In fact, if this problem were removed, the teacher could often ignore other "deviancies" in the child, since the child would at least be able to learn the course objectives and would stop bouncing around the room.

A behavioral analysis of this problem emphasizes that the child at present attends to a certain type of course material for a short time (entering behavior). The terminal behavior desired is having the child attend to such material for some specified longer time. When the typical classroom consequences of a child's (let's call him Johnny) short attention span are analyzed, they usually show aspects of the following:

1. Johnny attends to some task, at which time the teacher is happy that he is occupied, since now she can work with some other children. Thus Johnny is being ignored; the consequence of Johnny's working is to be ignored by the teacher.
2. Johnny stops working at the task and does something else, at which time the teacher reminds Johnny that he should be working and often takes him by the hand and leads him back to his work space. Thus the consequence of Johnny's not working is to receive the teacher's attention.

Looked at in this way, the first step in increasing Johnny's attention span is to have the teacher attend to his working behavior—not his inappropriate behavior. At first, the teacher will have to praise Johnny (or find some other effective reinforcer) for working for very short periods of time. The schedule of reinforcement here will be short intervals—very nearly continuous reinforcement. As the child begins to attend to his work for longer periods, the teacher can then lengthen the intervals between reinforcements. But consistent with the principles of intermittent reinforcement, she must attend to Johnny's appropriate behavior. By considering it a problem in reinforcement schedules, the teacher will be able to slowly shape Johnny's attention span.

TEACHER/STUDENT RATIOS

From the previous example, it is obvious that one teacher would not be able to deal effectively with a class of 30 Johnnys. Since Johnny needs to be on a continuous (or nearly continuous) schedule of reinforcement at first, it will be physically impossible for the teacher to spread herself around to more than a few such students. Except in the generally smaller classes for exceptional children, this fact is often ignored in schools today. Class size is usually determined for administrative convenience and not for the recognized educational needs of students and teachers.

We are not naive enough to expect that the schools will ever reduce the teacher/student ratio to some optimal level—it will probably always be less than optimal. What the teacher needs to do, therefore, is to recognize problems in terms of reinforcement, recognize his/her own limitations in providing more than a few students with nearly continuous reinforcement, and get help. Surprisingly, help is almost always available for the asking. Paid teacher aides and student teachers are one source. Parents as classroom helpers are another. Older or more advanced students in the school system are yet another. Finally, perhaps the least tapped resources are the underclassmen enrolled in teacher-education programs at local colleges and universities—students who are often only too happy to assist in classrooms. What all of these people can do, under a program managed by the teacher, is help to provide the properly scheduled reinforcement to shape desired behaviors.

CHAPTER FIVE
DISCRIMINATION AND GENERALIZATION

STUDY QUESTIONS

1. What is meant by discrimination training?
2. Define the following:
   a. discriminative stimulus (S^D or S+).
   b. inappropriate stimulus (S^Δ or S−).
3. What is the first step for the teacher in discrimination training?
4. What is stimulus generalization?
5. Describe the generalization gradient.
6. Why might a response that occurs at a high rate in one classroom occur at a low rate in another classroom?
7. How is discrimination learning related to our curriculum planning?

DISCRIMINATION

In the Kennedy Cottage behavior-modification program described earlier, a young girl named Susan tended to be very annoying to her counselors because of her rudeness. After some period of enduring this rudeness with great difficulty, the counselors decided to take a positive approach and reinforce social behaviors that were inconsistent with rudeness. The first step in their program consisted of giving points to Susan whenever she said "thank you." (A cottage store had previously been established so that children could earn points to spend on a variety of foods and drinks.) The counselors agreed to give Susan 20 points every time she made the correct response. Following establishment of the reinforcement contingency, every counselor cooperated in implementing it.

One week later, Susan was observed going from one counselor to another saying "thank you" and collecting her points. The effect of the reinforcement contingency was to increase the frequency of the response, but, because no one had trained Susan to discriminate the conditions under which the response was and was not appropriate, she said "thank you" inappropriately.

The basic goal of **discrimination training** is to increase the rate of correct responding in the presence of an appropriate stimulus and to decrease the rate of responding when this stimulus is absent. The appropriate stimulus is formally called a **discriminative stimulus** (often abbreviated S^D or S^+); sometimes it is called a cue. If the response is emitted in the presence of the S^D, it is reinforced.

When the appropriate stimulus (S^D) is absent or when some inappropriate stimulus is present, reinforcement is not made available. The presence of an inappropriate stimulus is called **S-delta** (S^Δ or S^-). Since the response is not reinforced when it occurs in the presence of S^Δ (it is being extinguished), responses in the presence of S^Δ will decrease or disappear as time progresses. However, responding in the presence of S^D is maintained because reinforcement *is* made available. When a subject consistently responds correctly in the presence of S^D and does not respond in the absence of S^D (the presence of S^Δ), it can be concluded that he has learned to make the discrimination.

The counselors' mistake in training Susan, then, was not having decided specifically *where* and *when* Susan's response of "thank you" should have been reinforced (such as on occasions in which someone did something for or gave something to Susan). In more technical language, they should have reinforced Susan's "thank you" response in the presence of S^D but not in the presence of S^Δ.

Dreikurs (1968) provides many examples of classroom problems to which discrimination analyses are applicable. One art teacher reported to him, for example, that her class became so noisy that she found it extremely difficult to give the assignment. After 4 weeks of increasing exasperation, the teacher became desperate and contrived a plan. The plan was that, if the children would pay attention during the first 15 minutes of class or whenever the teacher raised her hand, then the class could talk while working for the remainder of the class period. The teacher reported to Dreikurs that this was quite a successful procedure, and he praised it as being based on mutual respect and responsibility.

Of course the plan was based on mutual respect and responsibility: it was a sensible reinforcement contingency with a preferred activity as the reinforcer for a nonpreferred activity. In addition, the teacher provided a clear-cut discrimination situation. Her raised hand was used as an S^D to signal the occasion for quiet, attentive behavior. This, in turn, was reinforced by a period of talking while working. The absence of the raised hand, then, was the S^Δ (being quiet received no reinforcer). Situations like this are common in the schools, and a teacher's survival often depends on his ability to provide unambiguous S^Ds.

THE STUDENT'S ENTERING BEHAVIOR

The first task of a teacher in discrimination training is to determine whether the desired response can be performed or emitted by the student. If the response can be emitted, it can be reinforced in the presence of an S^D and ignored in the presence of S^Δ. If the subject cannot make the response, shaping procedures must be employed, using the techniques described earlier.

An important point to remember is that almost all unsuccessful discrimination training fails because training is not begun at a level consistent with the individual's initial capacity for responding.

After an individual's entering behavior for the desired response has been established to be at the appropriate level, discrimination training can start. At this point, discrimination training is begun in the manner we have outlined: a correct response is reinforced when it is emitted in the presence of the appropriate stimulus and not when it is emitted in the presence of an inappropriate stimulus.

Note that this is essentially what occurs in the learning of any concept. For instance, when a babbling child first utters the syllable "da," he is immediately showered with attention from adults who barrage him with such statements as "Say da-da." At this point the frequency of the syllable "da" will rise remarkably as adults reinforce this first approximation of "da-da." (Note, too, how imitating as a process is being reinforced.) Later, as the shaping goes on, the child will find that "da" is not an adequate response for reinforcement but that "da-da" is. Once "da-da" is emitted at a high rate, however, discrimination training begins: the child is reinforced for saying "da-da" when the father (or his picture) is present but not when he is absent. In fact, saying "da-da" in the presence of an S^Δ such as the milkman or a male friend of the family is actively discouraged.

STIMULUS GENERALIZATION

Responses that are recently learned are often initially emitted in all sorts of stimulus situations, as we found with Susan's saying "thank you" and the child's saying "da-da." As the parents begin to teach discrimination by reinforcing the child for saying "da-da" only when his father is present, the child is very likely to say "da-da" in the presence of other stimuli, such as other men. This tendency to emit the same response in the presence of several similar stimuli is called **stimulus generalization,** and the response is said to generalize from one stimulus to another.

THE GENERALIZATION GRADIENT

The more alike the original stimulus and the new stimuli are, the more frequently the response will be emitted in the presence of the new ones. For example, because the "da-da" response is being reinforced in the presence of the child's father and not reinforced in his absence, the child will often respond "da-da" in the presence of another man; but he will probably respond "da-da" somewhat less frequently in the presence of a woman, less frequently still in the presence of a child, and probably not at all in the presence of a dog. The curve that can be plotted from these frequencies is called a **generalization gradient,** and it demonstrates that the more similar a new stimulus is to the reinforced stimulus, the more frequently the response will be emitted in the presence of that stimulus.

Stimulus generalization is a common occurrence in learning to read. For example, teach a child who cannot yet read to say "man" to the printed stimulus MAN, and then provide him with these printed words several times in random order: MAN, MEN, WOMAN, BOY. If he responds "man" to more than the correct stimulus, you will probably find that his errors occur more frequently with similar than with dissimilar stimuli (with most errors occurring to MEN and the least to BOY). In responding "man" to stimuli other than MAN, the child is generalizing, and a graph plotting the frequency of occurrence of "man" to each stimulus would demonstrate the generalization gradient.

In the laboratory, stimulus generalization and the generalization gradient can be demonstrated more precisely by placing a hungry pigeon in a darkened experimental chamber with an illuminated disc or key on one wall of the chamber (for example, see Reese, 1966). By pecking the key, the pigeon can obtain a small quantity of grain. After the pigeon is trained to peck the key for food when the key is a certain color (say, yellow), food delivery is stopped. Then the color of the key is systematically varied over a wide range of the color spectrum. The order of presentation of the different colors may be randomized, but each color is presented for the same duration and number of times.

The next step is to count the responses recorded for each of the different colors. The typical finding is that amount of responding follows a highly regular pattern in relationship to the different hues. The greatest amount of key-pressing in this period in which food is not available occurs for the colors most similar to the original stimulus. As color of the key is changed to wavelengths further and further from the original color, responding decreases correspondingly. The curve made from response rates (the generalization gradient) is found to be a function of the different test wavelengths.

What is the significance of the generalization gradient? This gradient shows the presence of a mechanism by which the organism can respond appropriately to individual members of some response class to which it had never previously been exposed. Much of learning and experience in life has to do with identifying stimuli as members of classes, such as collies, poodles, and beagles as members of the class we call "dogs." This is a kind of cataloging process that saves us immeasurable degrees of error and helps us to master our environment more quickly.

GENERALIZABILITY

Just as it is important to teach discriminations, it is important to teach proper generalizations. It is hoped, for example, that certain behaviors and attitudes, such as practicing honesty and raising one's hand in class, taught and reinforced by only one teacher, will generalize to other teachers. Very often such behaviors do generalize, but sometimes cheating is reinforced and honesty is either extinguished or punished. In these cases it is not surprising that students learn to discriminate when cheating will and will not be reinforced—that is, in the presence of which discriminative stimulus (usually a teacher) cheating will be reinforced.

Unfortunately, there is no way to ensure that a desirable response that is reinforced and occurs at a high, stable rate in the presence of one stimulus situation will be made in the presence of another. The best way to control the response is to make certain that the same reinforcement contingencies operate in the various situations. That is, if two teachers enforce the same list of rules in the same way, they will likely find students behaving very similarly in both classrooms.

DISCRIMINATION LEARNING AND CURRICULUM PLANNING

Since discrimination and generalization are the basic processes in concept learning, any curriculum should be tied directly to the discriminations required. Learning to read, for example, requires many discriminations at various levels: among the shapes and sounds of individual letters, among combinations of letters, among sequences and classes of words, and so on. It is necessary to specify the prerequisites of each successive required behavior and to take each student through each level in the proper sequence. This means that each discrimination must be learned by each student before successive levels can be achieved or before separate discriminations (such as individual letters) can be chained into combinations.

There are many ways of teaching discriminations and many media in which they can occur, from programmed instruction and television to lectures and books and from errorless procedures to those that allow the student to make errors. In each case, the critical factors appear to be (1) how well the task has been structured, (2) whether the student has begun at the appropriate point, and (3) whether the child has been reinforced for learning the discriminations involved. When students fail to learn to read, for example, it is most often because one of these factors has not been fulfilled. Of the three, the first two are perhaps the most obvious. The third, however, involving reinforcement, deserves some comment.

In our zeal to teach a child the correct discriminations in sounding out words, we often attend solely to his errors. Thus it is not unusual for the teacher or parent to stand poised, waiting for the child's error so that it can be corrected. Although on the surface this procedure appears to be necessary, it can be very harmful, since it constitutes punishment for the child's honest attempts to read. In other words, in correcting the simple discriminations, we may be punishing the larger act—the child's attempt to obtain meaning from the printed word. This dilemma often arises because of our impatience with the slowness of the child's learning all of the discriminations involved. But we need to remember the overall goal. It would be foolish to teach a child one discrimination well but at the same time to have him lose all willingness to read. In this case generalizability of his skill would be at the very minimum. Therefore, although some methods of teaching certain discriminations may be better than others, the major consideration must be the effect of the procedure on shaping the subject toward the terminal objective.

CHAPTER SIX
DECREASING THE FREQUENCY OF A RESPONSE: EXTINCTION, PUNISHMENT, AND SOME ALTERNATIVES

STUDY QUESTIONS

1. What is extinction? How does it differ from conditioning?
2. If extinction were used to reduce the rate of swearing at home, why might swearing need to be extinguished on the playground as well?
3. Describe two times during extinction in which the response rate may increase. What should be done about these increases?
4. Why is punishment so commonly used to reduce the rate of a response? That is, what is the effect of punishment on the punisher?
5. What is the immediate effect of punishment on the behavior of the person who is punished?
6. What are some of the side effects of punishment?
7. What is meant by reinforcing an alternative to the undesirable response?
8. What is the difference between deprivation for punishment and deprivation for use later as a reward?
9. Describe the time-out-from-reinforcement technique.

EXTINCTION

Extinction as a process in both operant and respondent conditioning was introduced in Chapter II. At this point we shall extend the coverage of extinction using examples from operant conditioning, although many of the same points also hold for extinction of respondents.

The technique of reinforcement provides a fundamental way of increasing the frequency of a response. If a response rate has been increased because of its consequences—that is, if a response rate has been reinforced—it should be able to be decreased by nonreinforcement. In fact, the withholding of reinforcing agents does decrease the frequency of behavior. Another name for withholding reinforcement of a response is *extinction.*

Extinction occurs when a previously reinforced response is no longer reinforced. In the Kennedy Cottage program, for example, the rate of the "thank you" response of Susan was increased by following it with points exchangeable for store items and privileges. To extinguish that response, the Kennedy counselors had only to withhold the points. If points were, in fact, maintaining the "thank you" response rate, then, after several responses in which the points were not given, Susan's rate of saying "thank you" would have dropped to near zero. Saying "thank you" would have paid off no longer.

Actually, what the Kennedy counselors needed to do was train Susan to discriminate. To do this, they should have reinforced her "thank you" with points in the presence of S^D (such as when someone gave something to Susan). Then, in the presence of S^D, the rate of responding "thank you" would have been increased or maintained. At the same time, the counselors should have extinguished the "thank you" response in the presence of S^Δ. That is, if Susan said "thank you" at an inappropriate time, the response should not have been reinforced. Then, in the presence of S^Δ, the response rate would have eventually decreased to near zero, at which point discrimination training would be complete.

Consider how parents might use the principle of extinction to reduce the frequency of swearing in a child. First, they must identify the reinforcing stimuli that are maintaining the response. The other children in the family may laugh when the child emits a swear word. This laughing may be reinforcing the response. Thus, to extinguish the response, the parents will have to stop the laughing behavior of the other children (which may be a difficult problem in itself). But if the child emits a swear word and everyone ignores the response, thereby supplying no reinforcing stimulus, the cursing response will occur less and less frequently at home. The response will be undergoing extinction.

Extinction follows the same generalization gradient as conditioning does. Therefore, the less similar the stimulus situation, the less likely that the response that has undergone extinction in the presence of one stimulus situation will also be extinguished in the presence of another. What this means is that the child's cursing may be discontinued at home because it is not reinforced there. To reduce its frequency on the playground, however, it is necessary to apply extinction procedures there as well.

THE FRUSTRATION EFFECT AND SPONTANEOUS RECOVERY

Another point about extinction is that, in the very beginning, the response to be extinguished often becomes more frequent before it begins to become less frequent. Thus, in the process of withholding reinforcement from the swearing child, the parents may actually notice an increased rate of swearing. This probably occurs as a result of the child's *frustration* over not getting attention for a response he was accustomed to having reinforced. But if nonreinforcement is continued (that is, if the increased rate of swearing is ignored), the rate of swearing will eventually decrease.

After extinction procedures have been applied and the response rate has dropped to near zero for several days, the rate of the response may increase again. This increase of the response rate appears to be a *spontaneous recovery* of the previous habit, although the rate of the response is not usually so high as it was preceding extinction. If this recovery occurs, it is probably the result of the presence of an environmental cue (S^D) for the old behavior—a cue that was absent for a while. The fact that the response is emitted again can be seen as a test of the contingencies in effect; in other words, the child may be testing whether the rules of reinforcement have changed.

Remember during both of these temporary increases in response rate that they are natural occurrences and should be expected. What is needed is consistent withholding of reinforcement—continuation of extinction. More than one extinction session is needed to decrease the frequency of most behaviors, especially those that have been performed habitually for long periods of time.

PUNISHMENT

DIRECT EFFECTS OF PUNISHMENT

Punishment is probably the strongest and quickest way known for changing behavior. It is also associated with some of the most unpleasant or aversive experiences know to man. We use it to affect the behavior of others, but we are deeply offended when they use it on us.

Punishment is important to the punisher as well as to the punished. The act of punishing is commonly reinforced either by the removal of some annoyance (negative reinforcement) or by the attainment of something attractive (positive reinforcement). A boy may strike his little sister to stop her teasing or to take away her lollipop. In either case, the boy's success will increase his tendency to hit his sister in the future under similar conditions. Thus *the punisher is being operantly conditioned by the consequences of his behavior*—a sobering point to remember when you feel the urge to punish someone "for his own good." As the rat in the Skinner box said to his mate, "Boy, do I have this experimenter conditioned; every time I press this bar, he gives me a pellet of food."

The most direct way of punishing is to apply an **aversive stimulus** —a slap, a blow, a pinch, a kick—whenever some unwanted behavior is emitted (usually by some younger, weaker person). This aversive stimulus is often preceded by a warning—some threat of what is to come. A common laboratory procedure is to follow a light or sound with an electric shock. For example, a white rat pressing a lever steadily for food is stimulated with the noise of a buzzer for perhaps 10 seconds, after which he receives a strong shock from the lever or from the floor of his cage. With a few such pairings of buzz and shock, the buzz alone will stop the bar-pressing response and cause the animal to "freeze."

In our everyday lives, as in the animal laboratory, warning (discriminative) stimuli usually precede punishment. When a father has a certain expression on his face or when a mother speaks in a certain tone of voice, a child may recognize that a spanking is on the way. His ongoing behavior, like that of the laboratory rat, may be suppressed; if no avoidance is possible, he too may "freeze" until the spanking comes.

SIDE EFFECTS OF PUNISHMENT

Punishment may have unexpected outcomes. A child consistently ignored by his mother may learn that certain annoying acts, including tantrums, will get her attention and ultimately the object he may want, even though she spanks him for his "bad" behavior. At a later time the chances of tricks and tantrums will be increased rather than decreased by the attention he receives from his mother.

A study by Thomas, Becker, and Armstrong (1968) nicely demonstrates how stimuli typically considered aversive can have effects opposite to those intended. In this study the teacher's approval for appropriate behavior was withdrawn from a class of second-graders, with the result that disruptive behaviors increased in frequency. When the teacher tripled the number of critical comments directed at these disruptive behaviors, the disruptions increased further. It was only after the teacher reinstated approval responses that a stable low rate of disruptive behaviors occurred.

Another study demonstrated that effect in a different way. Spencer (1972) identified a class of behaviors he called "mouthing behaviors," defined as "touching of lips, teeth, or inner mouth area with objects such as pens, pencils, fingers, or candy" (pp. 3–4). This class of behaviors was chosen for study because of its relative neutrality in the classroom—that is, the three teachers in the first-grade classrooms that were studied neither rewarded nor punished these behaviors during the first week of baseline observations. At the start of the second week the teachers were asked to read a list of "don'ts" to the class (for example, "Do not put pens, pencils, or crayons into your mouth") and to disapprove verbally each time students were caught disobeying the new rules. The effect of the teachers' reprimands was to increase the frequency of mouthing behaviors above base line. A few weeks later the teachers were asked to verbally reinforce nonmouthing behaviors, such as by approving the termination of a mouthing behavior or by recognizing by name a child who was not engaged in such behavior. The effect of this procedure was to reduce the frequency of mouthing behavior to slightly below its original base rate.

Both the Thomas et al. (1968) and the Spencer (1972) studies demonstrate how a teacher can actually create unwanted behavior by a procedure that, to the teacher, appears to be punishing but is actually reinforcing. These studies support the observations about gum chewing reported in the Introduction. There is, in short, good evidence that reprimands, intended as a mild form of punishment to reduce the frequency of certain behaviors, actually increase the frequency of those behaviors.

Moderate punishment, perhaps in the form of physical slaps or spankings, detention after school, or traffic tickets, may suppress (reduce the frequency of) unacceptable behavior with apparent effectiveness, yet fail to produce a permanent change. In these cases we have the familiar discrimination learning: in the presence of the punisher (for example, a teacher or a policeman), we do not perform the unwanted behavior (passing notes or speeding); in the absence of the punisher, there is no change in the frequency of performance of the behavior.

In contrast to mild or moderate punishment, extreme punishment may have a longer-lasting effect, but it can lead to a wide variety of injurious physiological changes associated (through respondent conditioning) with emotional upset. For example, if a person is placed in a situation in which strong punishment cannot always be avoided by any response he emits and in which a high standard of some performance is required, many emotional outcomes may be expected. The palms of his hands may sweat, his pulse may beat faster, his adrenal glands may pour out hormones in profusion, and other signs of stress may also be observable. The more difficult the avoidance and the more aversive the consequences, the more disturbance we may look for. Bowel and bladder control may be lost, nausea and dizziness may be experienced, orientation in time and space may be destroyed, and general confusion may result. Long-time exposure to such conditions may even lead to ulcers, hypertension, disorders of breathing, certain kinds of skin disease, disturbance of sleep, the lowering of activity levels, impairment of skills, and the development of peculiar social behavior.

These responses become associated with conditioned stimuli and generalize to similar stimuli in the same way that reinforcement and extinction effects may generalize. Thus we find that a child who goes to a doctor and receives an injection not only screams and tries to avoid the doctor on subsequent occasions but reacts in the same way to a barber. Presumably, white coats, odors, or instruments have acted as conditioned stimuli for these physiological fear respondents (as well as discriminative stimuli for avoidance operants), and these responses have generalized to similar stimuli.

In short, punishment disrupts much more than the punished act, even though its short-term effect may be to reduce the rate of that act. However, punishment also often leads to long-term avoidance of the punisher as well as of objects or persons associated with him. Finally, punishment does not inform the punished person how he ought to behave in the future—that is, does not tell him what alternative responses will be reinforced. All in all, punishment is a dangerous way to control behavior.

ALTERNATIVES TO PUNISHMENT

In view of these effects of punishment, it would be nice to be able to conclude that punishment should never be used, that we should use instead the primary means of reducing the frequency of a response—namely, extinction. Unfortunately, some responses must be punished, because extinction will not work fast enough to be effective. An example of such a response is a child's running into the street. By the time a parent could reduce the rate of such behavior through nonreinforcement, the child's life might be extinguished.

REINFORCING ALTERNATIVE RESPONSES

At the same time, punishment may have the effect of reducing the frequency of the child's running into the street only when the parent is present (by discrimination learning). The solution to the problem, therefore, is teaching the child an alternative response and reinforcing it. Thus, if the child runs out into the street, he should be immediately reprimanded and returned to the sidewalk, but then he should be instructed in the correct method of crossing the street. This response should then be rewarded. In other words, a contingency should be introduced in which the correct response is rewarded by praise and by the child's being allowed to go across the street, while incorrect responses are not rewarded in those ways. This kind of punishment, used in connection with reinforcement of some alternative response (often a response incompatible with the undesirable response), is a much more effective technique for eliminating such behaviors than is either punishment, extinction, or reinforcement used alone.

There are many behaviors we frequently decide to punish. Often we *feel* that we should punish them because we have lost control of ourselves and are being shaped by our students or children, whose goal, perhaps, is to make us angry (see, for example, Dreikurs, 1968); nevertheless, the perception is real, and we must act. This is the point at which it is useful to have a habitual mode of punishing the inappropriate behavior and establishing favorable conditions for reinforcing appropriate behaviors at the same time. Merely punishing will first of all not work in the long run to reduce the behavior problem, but it will more than likely reinforce the behavior you want to eliminate. This is especially true in classrooms of adolescents in which one of the favorite activities reinforced by peers is upsetting the teacher. Thus a habitual punishment mode by the teacher is usually a good indication that the teacher is being shaped by the students and that therefore the latter are in control of the class—an opposite conclusion to that usually drawn by strict disciplinarians.

If the teacher truly wants to have control over his students, he must reinforce desirable behaviors and condition positive emotions toward himself and his curriculum. In Friedenberg's words:

> But influence does not mean pushing people around; it means leading them to want to do what you want them to do . . . it requires real awareness of what other people need and some skill in helping them get it. More than anything else, it requires a clear understanding of what is going on and how things actually work. An influential person is no bully; he is a sculptor who works in the medium of human situations. He must respect his tools, his materials, and his market [1959, p. 59].

PUNISHMENT VERSUS DEPRIVATION

Punishment is commonly confused with deprivation, from which it should be clearly distinguished. The essence of deprivation lies in making an object or activity unavailable to an animal or person in order to use it later as a reward. A rat that has just been fed or a little girl who has just consumed a box of candy is a poor subject for learning to press a lever or perform any other act for which food pellets or sweets are used as reinforcers. Of course, the effect is very different after the subjects go a period of time without eating.

For some persons, the usual social reinforcers are not enough to maintain their behavior. A withdrawn, psychotic patient in a chronic-care ward may be totally unaffected by things that would be rewarding to a normal person. In such cases it may be necessary to resort to deprivation in order to shape the pattern of response desired. Everyone must sleep and everyone must eat and everyone must drink. If nothing else can be found, a psychotic's behavior may be influenced by withholding food or water or sleep long enough to use it as a reinforcer. This deprivation, even for a short period, may seem excessively cruel, but it is surely less cruel than allowing him to live out his life in total dependency and inaction when a more rewarding existence is possible.

A less satisfactory use of deprivation is often practiced by parents when they withhold some object or activity from children as a form of punishment. To send a boy to bed without his supper is far less effective and satisfying to all concerned than the same deprivation would be if receiving supper were made contingent on more acceptable behavior. Thus the boy should be told that, as soon as he completes his task, he may have supper.

Traditional classroom grading practices provide another example of punishment, as contrasted with one suggested use of deprivation. If a student does not learn the objectives of the course to the required level, he typically receives an undesirable grade (such as a D or an F). The teacher is attempting to punish the student's behavior in this way, but he does so at the expense of not getting the student motivated to do the work. How much better it would be to give the student more opportunities to learn the material and therefore to receive a rewarding grade! Such grading procedures exist in schools that use what is called criterion-referenced or mastery testing; they are discussed in more detail in the next chapter.

TIME OUT FROM REINFORCEMENT

Brown and Tyler (1967) have presented results on the use of brief isolation as a group-control device for institutionalized delinquents. The subjects were 15 boys from 13 to 15 years of age who were all committed by the State for auto theft, assault, incorrigibility, sex offenses, and the like. The experimental plan was to attack a problem that was considered significant by counseling staff, using a general technique that could be applied to all children in the living unit.

The problem concerned how the boys behaved around the pool table in the day room. They often engaged in behaviors such as breaking rules, throwing or hitting one another with pool cues, scuffling, bothering other players, bouncing balls on the floor, kibitzing, and arguing.

The control technique employed to weaken these behaviors consisted of isolating the offender in a small "time-out" room. An 11-minute time-out period was used for each offense. The offender was simply removed from the day room without any show of emotion to the time-out room and locked up for the 11-minute period.

The first phase of the investigation was carried out over a 7-week period. This consisted of instituting the time-out procedure. Whenever an offense occurred, a tally was made for the records. The second phase was carried out over a 13½-week period. During this phase the time-out procedure was discontinued, but the staff did employ techniques for verbal persuasion to reduce or eliminate the same undesirable behaviors. The third phase lasted for 20 weeks. This was simply a return to the original time-out procedure.

The results were as follows. Cumulative records of offenses compiled on a weekly basis for each individual boy showed that when the time-out procedure was instituted there was a significant decrease in pool-table offenses. When the time-out procedure was removed in phase 2, offenses began to rise rapidly for every individual observed. The reintroduction of the time-out procedure led again to a very sharp reduction of offenses. This reduction was noted for every individual.

Other investigators have used this technique with the addition of allowing the person to return early to the situation from which he was removed as a reward for good behavior while in the time-out situation. Similar procedures are used by parents or teachers who, when their children are misbehaving, remove them to their rooms with the suggestion that "you may return whenever you can behave properly." This technique emphasizes the positive side of the behavior: while you are removed from the possibility of earning reinforcement for the present, making a certain response will be reinforced.

Here again the emphasis is on the positive behaviors. There is also an added benefit: since the parents remove themselves from situations in which endless arguments or reprimands might ensue, there can be no accidental reinforcement of the behavior that is not wanted. A nonemotional removal of the child from the situation to a time-out room with a specification of the conditions under which the child may return can be very effective. It is effective because it takes the child away from any possible reinforcement; more importantly, it gives the parent or teacher another chance to avoid excessive anger and to attend to appropriate behavior. For many adults this is a major shift in their mode of responding to children. The time-out procedure allows them the opportunity to practice attending to appropriate behavior, and herein lies the real strength of the technique.

CHAPTER SEVEN
CONDITIONING AND A PHILOSOPHY OF INSTRUCTION

STUDY QUESTIONS

1. How are the principles of conditioning related to each of the following roles of a teacher?
   a. establishing instructional objectives.
   b. structuring the task.
   c. accounting for entering behavior.
   d. providing instruction.
   e. assessing learning.
2. What does "adapting instruction to individual differences" mean, according to the principles of conditioning presented in this book?
3. What statement might reflect a reinforcement theorist's philosophy of education?
4. Why should teachers be more concerned with good behaviors than with bad? Give an example.

CONDITIONING AND INSTRUCTION

In any situation in which learning is expected to occur, the teacher must be concerned with (1) instructional objectives, (2) the structure of the task itself, (3) the student's entering behavior with regard to the task, (4) the actual instructional procedures used, and (5) assessment of whether the instructional objectives have been met. Although teaching involves more than conditioning, good teaching procedures incorporate the principles of conditioning that have been presented in this book. In this chapter we shall relate the principles of conditioning to these five integral parts of teaching.

INSTRUCTIONAL OBJECTIVES

One of the major functions of a teacher is to facilitate learning in or by students. Facilitation of learning is accomplished in many ways, but all methods begin with a specification of the goal that is to be reached. Specifying the goal is defining an instructional objective or series of objectives. What those objectives are and how they are defined influence the rest of the teacher's functions and therefore the student's learning. Objectives are useful only to the extent that they specify the behaviors (attitudes, values, or responses) the students will be capable of on completion of instruction. In other words, the objectives must be specified in behavioral terms—that is, in terms of the performances the student should be capable of or the activity preferences the students should have. Since these terminal behaviors are expected, the objectives automatically suggest the type of assessment that can be used to evaluate whether the objectives have been attained by each student.

This emphasis on clearly stated behavioral objectives is a primary part of the operant-conditioning model. However, unlike the experimenter who defines the objectives when shaping pigeons, a teacher does not have to define objectives independently of the students. In some cases, of course, this may be the only reasonable procedure. But in many cases —many more than educators currently admit to—it would be very reasonable to allow students major responsibility for establishing the course objectives. In practice, this could become a kind of contractual arrangement between each student and the teacher, with each contract specifying the instructional objective to be attained by the completion of the period of study. More imaginative use of such procedures not only would bring individualized instruction into the classroom but would go a long way toward making school relevant to life.

Notice that there is nothing inherently wrong, from a conditioning point of view, with allowing democracy to operate to establish objectives. Moreover, as we indicated in Chapter III, there is no necessary incompatibility between this approach and more cognitive approaches, which emphasize learning difficult to specify in behavioral terms. This is because we can set short-range objectives that, once attained, may suggest new objectives to be set. The important point is that the teacher must be able to assess whether students are achieving the objectives.

TASK ANALYSIS

Once the instructional objectives and the student behaviors that will satisfy those objectives have been specified, the next step is to analyze the structure and requirements of the task. This may be one of the most important functions of the teacher: to structure the material in such a way as to facilitate learning. Thus complex principles (for example, "reinforcement should be contingent on the occurrence of an appropriate response") must be broken down into their component concepts or subprinciples ("reinforcement," "contingent," "response"), understanding of which is prerequisite to understand the superordinate principle. Each of the prerequisite concepts must also be analyzed into its components. For instance, "reinforcement" is composed of the following subprinciples and concepts: "a stimulus that follows a response and that has defined effects on the subsequent strength or rate of the response." In turn, "response," "stimulus," "response strength," and "response rate" must be analyzed for their components. This task-analysis process could be carried on downward until recognition of words and of the letters of the alphabet was specified as a necessary prerequisite. This discussion is based on the Gagné-Paradise (1961) analysis of the structure of content materials for acquiring knowledge; note how consistent their theory is with the reinforcement principles involved in shaping.

ENTERING BEHAVIOR

Once the task has been structured, the teacher's next function in facilitating learning is to start each student at the appropriate point in that structure. It makes no sense to begin teaching about reinforcement, for example, if the student does not know the prerequisite principles of "response," "stimulus," and so on (just as it would make no sense to require a pigeon to turn a circle, ring a bell, and then peck a key in succession for reinforcement before it learned to peck a key alone). The teacher is obligated, therefore, to be concerned with what each student already knows about the material, beginning instruction at that point by briefly reviewing the prerequisite concepts to refresh the student's memory. Again, this is directly parallel to the procedure used to shape responses.

Less obvious but equally important aspects of the concept of entering behavior have to do with the student's developmental readiness for the concepts, as well as his motivation or interest in learning them at that time. At various developmental stages, children may learn the same concepts with greater ease and with a greater subsequent amount of understanding than they might have at earlier stages. Harlow (1959) demonstrated this quite convincingly in studies with monkeys, showing that in general the rate at which the monkeys learned to solve similar problems (learning to learn) was highly related to their age. The older the monkey, the more rapid the learning. More important, the less mature monkeys trained to solve these problems never caught up with the old monkeys; there was a kind of permanent impairment in the eventual amount of proficiency these monkeys developed in solving these problems.

Jensen (1969) showed another side of this same problem in a description of his attempts to teach his 5-year-old daughter to play chess. He first analyzed the task into the hierarchy of skills necessary to play the game. He then proceeded to start at her level of entering behavior, which was categorizing the chess pieces into whites and blacks, a task she learned in one trial. Then she learned the names of each of the chess pieces, which took only a few trials. Jensen continued teaching his daughter correct placement of the pieces on the board and the rules governing movement of each piece. She learned all of this in a few days, finding it fun, so that she was eager to continue. But when they attempted a game of chess, using all of these subordinate rules, she was not able to function at this level. Although reinforcement (that is, stimuli that maintained responses in previous learning) was given for approximations to good moves, there was an immediate motivational slump that not only affected her willingness to play further but that also was reflected in the apparent deterioration of the skills previously learned. To avoid coercion, Jensen discontinued the lessons for a year, after which time his daughter quickly caught on and found the game sufficiently interesting to want to play every evening.

These examples demonstrate the effects of being required to learn tasks that are too complex for the maturational state of the student. Reinforcing the child's efforts can be fruitful in getting him to spend more time at the task; but if spending that time results in continued failures because the child lacks the cognitive or perceptual skills, then the result will be frustration and withdrawal from the situation. Continued coercion, such as is often the case in schools in which all students must move at the same pace, can have unfortunate long-range effects.

It is at this major juncture that cognitive-developmental theories, such as Piaget's (see, for example, Flavell, 1963), complement the behavioral principles we have presented in this book. In other words, these different theoretical positions are not necessarily adversaries. Together they can begin to provide us with a comprehensive understanding of behavior.

One final point about reinforcing attending behavior. It is widely assumed that the more time a student attends to a task, the more he will learn. From this assumption it follows that reinforcement that is given contingent on attention will improve school performance. However, recent studies by Ferritor and associates (1972) suggest that the relationship between task attention and correctness of performance is not that simple. In their studies of arithmetic-drill exercises in third-graders, they found that (1) reinforcing attending behavior alone increased attending and decreased disruptions but had little effect on correctness of work; (2) reinforcing correctness of work alone increased accuracy with little positive effect on attending and disruptions; and (3) reinforcing both attending and correctness was necessary to improve accuracy, increase attention, and decrease disruptions. Thus reinforcement effects may be more specific than we would hope for, and, in order to understand the behavior, strict attention must be paid to the actual reinforcement contingency operating.

Returning now to entering behavior and the reinforcing of successive approximations to the desired terminal behaviors, we see the necessity for one additional option. If a teacher in all his zeal to get his students to want to learn something finds a student turning off and can find no way of motivating the student short of coercion, it may be better to allow the child the freedom not to do the work. In the long run, forcing the child to work on something he sees no use for or cannot comprehend may have quite damaging consequences. This is not to say that the teacher should give up on the child and ignore him. It means that the teacher should find out where the student is and what his interests are in an attempt to establish bridges to the curriculum.

INSTRUCTIONAL PROCEDURES

We have traced the teacher's functions through stating objectives, performing a task analysis, and accounting for each student's entering behavior. The next function is the actual instruction itself—the presentation of the material through lectures, textbooks, films, programmed instruction, or whatever. Here the important point is to take each student from his present entering behavior to achievement of whatever objectives have been established to assure that he not only learns the concepts but learns to like the material. As has been stressed before, if not enough time to finish is allowed a student who is spending his time actively learning, the student feels the pressure of time. With repeated unsuccessful attempts to complete the material, a student can begin to feel frustrated and inferior, the effect of which will be that his appropriate behavior will decrease in frequency (since it is being punished or, at the least, extinguished). On the other hand, if a student is forced to move too slowly, he can become bored and restless, feelings that set the conditions for him to dislike the material, as well as to become a behavior problem.

The interaction of individual differences and instructional procedures. There is much concern at present with finding the right teaching method for each subgroup of students who are alike in a given trait or ability. The current lingo calls it "the individual differences (or aptitude) by instructional treatment interaction" (see, for example, Cronbach & Snow, 1969). For researchers in this field the problem is to find a particular instructional procedure that is maximally effective for one subgroup of individuals (for example, "culturally disadvantaged") and a different method that works best for another subgroup of individuals ("nondisadvantaged"). For many technical reasons, which we shall ignore here, there have yet to be found methods that work well for one group but not for another and that yield results sufficiently important to be used by schools.

For our purposes, however, all of this talk about classifying individuals into subgroups and then giving all those within the subgroup the same treatment is not dealing with individuals at all. We would still have to allow each student to go at his own rate, we would still want some of the students to try other methods if they were so inclined, and so forth. Thus the search for this "individual difference by method interaction" is pointless in any real sense of what teachers should do in the schools.

Instead of searching for those students who learn best by rote memorization, say, and giving them a program based mainly on rote learning, we teachers should provide the students with the best instructional packages we can—a cafeteria of approaches to include rote memory, inductive learning, and anything else we can find. If we make all of this available to the students, allow them to try whatever they want, and encourage them in whatever they try, we shall be adapting better to individuals than we shall be by subgrouping students. At the present time this is all we know how to do with regard to individual differences. *It is also all that is necessary to adapt education to individual differences.*

PERFORMANCE ASSESSMENT AND GRADING PRACTICES

The final function of a teacher with regard to instruction is to assess whether each student has met the instructional objectives. There are of course many ways of doing this, but all of them should be based on the particular behaviors required as specified in the instructional objectives. The important point to remember is that the teacher's task is *to provide each student with the opportunity to achieve the instructional objectives.*

Traditional grading practices, however, are competitive (the technical name is norm-referenced) in that the performance of one student is evaluated in terms of the performance of other students. As Gentile (1971a) argues, *"Competitive grading practices are sadistic, unethical, statistically unsound, and irrelevant to the course objectives."* Competitive assessment procedures are sadistic because they pit one student against another, discouraging cooperation. In addition, such procedures are based on the assumption that everyone cannot or should not succeed in the course—an unethical assumption in a country in which the school's purpose is to give each child the basic skills and attitudes that will allow him to define success for himself. Competitive grading practices are statistically unsound because any test that is designed to rank students differentially—even a perfectly reliable test, of which there are none—cannot discriminate between a score that falls into the area receiving one grade (say, 90% = A) and the closest score falling into the area receiving an adjacent grade (say, 89% = B). Thus the competitive grading process is arbitrary.

Most important of all, competitive grading practices are irrelevant to the instructional objectives, since concern should be with *each student's* achieving the objectives. For each student who succeeds, therefore, the teacher may take credit; for each who fails, the teacher must also accept the blame and start over to help him succeed.

The answer, then, is to assess and grade noncompetitively in what is technically called criterion-referenced assessment (see Block, 1971, or Bloom, 1968, for examples of mastery-testing procedures). In this criterion-referenced procedure each student is evaluated in relation to the course objectives, the criterion for which he must demonstrate mastery independently of the performance of other students. Combining mastery learning with criterion-referenced assessment suggests further that, if the student fails to achieve the criterion on the first trial, he should be assisted in learning the material and allowed to try again. In fact, he must be considered to be in the process of learning—not to have failed—any time he has not yet mastered the material. Only in this way can assessment procedures work with, instead of against, the instructional procedures to develop the skills and attitudes specified in the teacher's instructional objectives.

A POSITIVE, SUPPORTIVE ENVIRONMENT

At the outset of this text we said that the reinforcement principles to be presented emphasize a positive, supporting environment, and indeed they do. The basic underlying principle of this text, reflected in the examples, is that desirable responses can be shaped and maintained through reinforcement of those responses. A kind of corollary of this principle is that undesirable responses are maintained by the same reinforcing consequences; therefore, to reduce their frequency, nonreinforcement (or moderate punishment), along with reinforcement of an alternative appropriate response, should occur.

Since the responsibility for the rates of various behaviors has been placed clearly on the environmental consequences that produce such behaviors, it is easy to understand why reinforcement theorists reflect a philosophy that places the praise or blame on teachers for the success or failure of their students. Actually, it is only fair. If teachers want to be considered responsible for their successful students, they must also be considered responsible for their unsuccessful students.

This is not to imply that behavior is totally or even mainly determined by environmental factors or that a certain teacher must be responsible for the mistakes of parents, other teachers, or peers. It does mean, however, that the teacher cannot hide behind those factors as an excuse for failure to motivate a child to succeed in his class. If a poor student is considered to be the responsibility of previous significant others, then a successful student should be also. This logic would lead to the conclusion that any teacher has about zero effect on any student.

While many critics of educational practices would like us to believe that teachers have virtually no effect on children, this is a pessimistic view. Anyone who goes into teaching with such a view of his potential effect on students should retire before he starts!

A teacher must believe that he can significantly affect the lives of the students with whom he is involved. Translated into behavioral terms, this means that a teacher must believe and be able to show evidence that all of his students have learned at least the basic objectives the course was designed to teach. More important, the teacher must recognize that possibly the most significant part of his interaction with students is his effect on such noncontent areas as work habits and experiences of success.

What does this mean in concrete terms? A third-grade student announced to his parents one day that he had had it with good behavior in class. It did not pay off either in attention from the teacher or in respect from the other students. For 3 years he completed his assignments quickly without making trouble. What did it get him? Additional assignments. The boys who did not do their assignments or made trouble often had the teacher's attention and never seemed to get additional assignments. His solution was to stop working quickly, stop identifying with the teacher, and start having some fun.

This particular student is very perceptive, and he has put his finger on probably the basic problem in education: most teachers ignore students until they do something wrong. This emphasis has to be reversed. Teachers have to see that good, desirable, normal behaviors are those on which attention should be placed. Classroom control, in other words, has to be conceived as reinforcement for positive behaviors, not as disciplinary measures for problem behaviors. *Instead of catching the students being bad, catch them being good.* With this emphasis many disciplinary and motivational problems can be prevented, and the classroom atmosphere will be more pleasant for all involved.

With regard to work habits, for example, if a certain amount of work is required, then completion of that work should be reinforced. A student who completes the work in 10 minutes, therefore, should have the rest of the period free for some activity he would enjoy doing. Such an approach, we are convinced, would increase the output of all members of the class, since there would be some payoff attached to being a hard-working, nondistracted student. We suspect that there would be few motivation or discipline problems in such a class.

Try it. You have nothing to lose but your behavior problems.

APPENDIX

A CHECKLIST FOR ASSESSING WHETHER THE MAIN PRINCIPLES OF THIS BOOK ARE BEING PRACTICED

As was stated in the last chapter, good teaching involves more than the behavioral principles described in this book. In fact it may never be possible to specify exactly what traits or qualities define a good teacher as opposed to a poor one. Nevertheless, a number of competencies can be specified that most certainly will help a teacher to achieve the kind of positive, supportive environment we advocate. We offer the following list of questions as a checklist to help teachers assess themselves or others with regard to the principles of this book. The list is, of course, nonexhaustive, but it is offered to summarize the course principles and to stimulate other questions about the application of these ideas to classrooms.

1. Have the instructional objectives been identified?
   a. Are instructional objectives translated into learning tasks?
   b. Can progress in accomplishing these tasks be objectively assessed?
   c. Has the teacher developed effective measures for determining mastery of the learning task?
2. Have the tasks associated with instructional objectives been analyzed into their component parts?
   a. Have the prerequisites to succeed in accomplishing the tasks been defined for the students?
   b. What is the entering behavior of each student with respect to mastery of the prerequisite skills?
3. How does the teacher attempt to motivate students to master the tasks defined?
   a. Does the teacher define consequences associated with mastery of the learning task?
   b. When a student does master the learning task, are there any positive consequences for his efforts?

c. If a student does not master the material to criterion level, does the teacher reinforce his partial success?
d. Does the teacher provide the student with feedback about his degree of success in achieving the task?
e. Does the teacher make efforts to ensure that all students master the task?

4. What is the nature of the teacher-student interaction?
a. Are students reinforced for contributing to the class?
b. Are students given opportunities to assist one another?
c. Are students reinforced for assisting one another?
d. Do students voluntarily contribute to the class?
e. Does the teacher attend primarily to the appropriate behaviors of the students?

5. What classroom assessment is used by the teacher?
a. Are students assessed in relation to their individual progress toward instructional goals?
b. Does the teacher use data on student progress to evaluate and improve the instructional methods?
c. Does the teacher provide relatively immediate feedback of results to the student?
d. Does the teacher indicate what elements of task performance have been accomplished satisfactorily?
e. Is the student given additional opportunities following initial feedback to master material that was not adequately learned?
f. Is feedback to students a continuing part of the instructional process?
g. Does the teacher solicit class evaluations from students?

6. How does the teacher involve the class with the learning process?
a. Are students given choices regarding study content?
b. Are students allowed to achieve learning objectives at differing rates?
c. Are students who have clearly mastered instructional objectives used to assist others?

GLOSSARY

Aversive stimulus. An unpleasant stimulus, such as a slap, blow, loud noise, or electric shock.

Baseline data. Same as *Base rate.*

Base rate. A measure of the naturally occurring frequency of a response before any attempt has been made to change it.

Conditioned reinforcer. Same as *Secondary reinforcer.*

Conditioned stimulus. A stimulus that was neutral before conditioning began but became capable of eliciting the response after being paired with an unconditioned stimulus.

Conditioning. A procedure in which an increase in the frequency of response occurs because a stimulus is paired with the response.

Consequence. The stimulus that follows a response.

Contingent reinforcement. The presentation of a reinforcing stimulus only if the correct response has been made.

Continuous reinforcement. The procedure of reinforcing every correct response.

Deprivation. (a) The process of withholding a stimulus so that it can later be used as a reinforcer. (b) The length of time the stimulus has been unavailable.

Discrimination training. The procedure of increasing the rate of responding in the presence of one stimulus and decreasing it in the presence of another.

Discriminative stimulus (S^D). The particular stimulus in the presence of which a correct response is likely to be reinforced.

Entering behavior. The specific behaviors the student can perform in relation to the hierarchy of skills required by the task. Knowing the student's entering behavior allows the teacher to start the student at the point in the curriculum at which the material will be neither too easy nor too difficult.

Extinction. In operant conditioning, the process of withholding reinforcement following performance of an operant; in respondent conditioning, the process of withholding the unconditioned stimulus following the presentation of the conditioned stimulus. Its usual effect is to reduce the strength or frequency of the response.

Fixed-interval (FI) schedule. An interval schedule in which reinforcement is given for the next correct response after a fixed amount of time since the last reinforcement.

Fixed-ratio (FR) schedule. A ratio schedule in which a fixed number of responses must be emitted before reinforcement is given.

Generalization. Same as *Stimulus generalization.*

Generalization gradient. The curve of response frequencies which shows that the more similar a stimulus is to the original S^D, the more likely the response will be performed in its presence.

Imitation. The procedure whereby an observer performs the behavior that he has seen some other person (the model) perform.

Imitative behavior. The behavior performed by an observer as a result of witnessing the behavior of some other person (a model).

Incompatible behavior. Behavior that is opposed to the behavior of interest. Examples of incompatible behaviors are competing and cooperating, hoarding and sharing, paying attention and being inattentive.

Instructional objectives. Specific performances stated in terms of observable behaviors that students are expected to acquire through instructional procedures.

Intermittent reinforcement. Same as *Partial reinforcement.*

Interval schedule. A reinforcement schedule in which reinforcement is contingent on the amount of time that has passed since the last reinforcement.

Model. In imitation, the person whose behavior is imitated.

Negative reinforcement. The removal of an aversive stimulus as a consequence of the performance of an operant response. Its effect is to increase or maintain the rate of the response.

Noncontingent reinforcement. The presentation of a reinforcing stimulus whether or not the correct response has been made.

Objectivity. An expression of facts with the minimum amount of distortion, prejudice, and interpretation.

Observer. In imitation, the person who witnesses the behavior of a model.

Operant. A response for which no eliciting stimulus can be found but whose rate is determined by its consequences (the stimuli that follow). Such a response is usually called "purposeful" and accounts for most of human behavior.

Partial reinforcement. A reinforcement schedule in which reinforcement is provided only after some, not all, of the correct responses.

Performance assessment. Evaluation of the student's progress through the material relative to the instructional objectives set for that particular student.

Positive reinforcement. The use of a (reinforcing) stimulus to increase or maintain the rate or frequency of an operant response.

Preferred activity. A type of secondary or conditioned reinforcer that consists of activities or behaviors people like to engage in.

Primary reinforcement. (a) A primary reinforcer. (b) The process of rewarding an operant response with a primary reinforcer.

Primary reinforcer. A stimulus that is rewarding because it fulfills some basic biological need (for example, food, water, or sleep).

Punishment. The procedure of applying an aversive stimulus to the subject as a consequence of his behavior. Its usual effect is to decrease temporarily the rate of responding.

Rate of response. Same as *Response frequency.*

Ratio schedule. A reinforcement schedule in which reinforcement is contingent on the number of responses performed, no matter how long it takes to emit the response.

Reinforcement. (a) The process of reinforcing or rewarding a response by following it with a reinforcer. (b) A reinforcer.

Reinforcement contingency. A rule stating which responses are to be reinforced.

Reinforcement schedule. A statement or rule that specifies how many or what proportion of the correct responses will be reinforced.

Reinforcer. A reinforcing stimulus.

Reinforcing stimulus. (a) A stimulus that comes after a response has been made and that increases the rate or frequency of that response. (b) A reward.

Resistance to extinction. The ability of a response to maintain its previous frequency when it is no longer reinforced.

Respondent. A response that follows a stimulus and is elicited by it as a reflex.

Response. An act that can be described as a single operation. The act can be as simple as a reflex or as complicated as the operation of walking or talking.

Response frequency. A description of how often a response occurs in some period of time.

Satiation. The process of making a stimulus excessively available so that it is no longer reinforcing.

S-delta (S^{Δ}). The particular stimulus that represents an occasion on which a response is not reinforced, in contrast to S^D, which represents the occasion on which the response will likely be reinforced.

Secondary reinforcer. A stimulus, such as money or praise, that is reinforcing because it has been paired with (or is exchangeable for) a primary reinforcer.

Shaping. The procedure of reinforcing successively closer approximations of the desired behavior in order to teach a new response.

Social reinforcer. A type of secondary or conditioned reinforcer that is provided by interaction with another person. Examples are smiles and praise.

Stimulus. An environmental event to which an animal or person is sensitive.

Stimulus generalization. The finding that a response originally reinforced in the presence of one stimulus (S^D) will also occur in the presence of other similar stimuli.

Successively closer approximations. Responses that are getting closer and closer to the desired behavior. These responses are reinforced in order to shape more complex responses out of simple responses.

Target behavior. The particular behavior, defined very specifically, that is of concern and is therefore to be observed and perhaps changed.

Task analysis. A structuring of the instructional material to be learned in terms of the hierarchy of skills and prerequisites needed at the various stages of learning the task.

Time out from reinforcements. A technique for reducing the frequency of undesirable behaviors by moving the subject from the situation in which reinforcements are available to a situation in which they are not available.

Time sampling. An observational technique in which selected aspects of behavior are observed and counted within short time intervals sampled throughout days or weeks.

Token. A type of secondary or conditioned reinforcer that is a physical or countable item, such as money or course grades.

Token economy. A small social system in which reinforcement in the form of some kind of token is provided immediately following the performance of desired responses by its members.

Unconditioned response. A response that is automatically elicited by a stimulus; a reflex. Also called a *Respondent.*

Unconditioned stimulus. A stimulus that comes before and elicits or causes a response (the response is called a respondent or unconditioned response).

Variable-interval (VI) schedule. An interval schedule in which reinforcement is contingent on performance of the next correct response following passage of the average of some predetermined amount of time.

Variable-ratio (VR) schedule. A ratio schedule in which reinforcement is contingent on performance of the average of some predetermined number of responses.

Vicarious reinforcement. In imitation, the procedure of reinforcing a response made by a model, with the result of increasing the frequency of that response by an observer who has not been directly reinforced for making the response.

REFERENCES

Baer, D. M., Peterson, R. F., & Sherman, J. A. The development of imitation by reinforcing behavior similarity to a model. *Journal of Experimental Analysis of Behavior,* 1967, **10,** 405–416.

Bandura, A. Social learning through imitation. In M. R. Jones (Ed.), *Nebraska symposium on motivation.* Lincoln: University of Nebraska Press, 1962. Pp. 211–269.

Bandura, A. *Principles of behavior modification.* New York: Holt, Rinehart & Winston, 1969.

Bandura, A., & Walters, R. H. *Social learning and personality development.* New York: Holt, Rinehart & Winston, 1963.

Block, J. H. (Ed.) *Mastery learning: Theory and practice.* New York: Holt, Rinehart & Winston, 1971.

Bloom, B. S. Learning for mastery. *Evaluation Comment,* 1968, **1**(2).

Brown, G. D., & Tyler, V. O., Jr. The use of swift, brief isolation as a group control device for institutionalized delinquents. *Behavior Research and Therapy,* 1967, **5,** 1–9.

Cronbach, L. J., & Snow, R. E. Individual differences in learning ability as a function of instructional variables: Final report. Office of Education, ERIC Document No. ED 029001, 1969.

Dreikurs, R. *Psychology in the classroom.* New York: Harper & Row, 1968.

Ferritor, D. E., Buckholdt, D., Hamblin, R. L., & Smith, L. The noneffects of contingent reinforcement for attending behavior on work accomplished. *Journal of Applied Behavior Analysis,* 1972, **5,** 7–17.

Ferster, C. B., & Perrott, M. C. *Behavior principles.* New York: Appleton-Century-Crofts, 1968.

Flavell, J. H. *The developmental psychology of Jean Piaget.* Princeton, N.J.: Van Nostrand, 1963.

Franklin, B. In B. F. Skinner, Operant reinforcement of prayer. *Journal of Applied Behavior Analysis,* 1969, **2,** 247.

Frazier, B. H. Design of a microeconomy system for correcting delinquent behavior patterns in institutionalized children. Paper presented at the conference of Behavioral Engineering in Therapeutic Environments, Walter Reed Army Medical Center, Washington, D.C., January 31, 1969.

Frazier, T. W., Gentile, J. R., & Morris, M. C. *Classroom applications of reinforcement principles.* Dubuque, Iowa: Kendall/Hunt, 1970.

Friedenberg, E. Z. *The vanishing adolescent.* New York: Dell, 1959.

Gagné, R. M., & Paradise, N. E. Abilities and learning sets in knowledge acquisition. *Psychological Monographs,* 1961, **75** (14, Whole No. 518).

Gentile, J. R. Pigeons, pecking orders and public schools. Unpublished manuscript, State University of New York at Buffalo, 1972.

Gentile, J. R. Toward excellence in teaching: Grading practices. Unpublished manuscript, State University of New York at Buffalo, 1971. (a)

Gentile, J. R. Educational psychology principles applied to educational psychology courses. Paper presented at the 79th Annual Convention of the American Psychological Association, Washington, D.C., September 7, 1971. (b)

Gentile, J. R., & Lawson, H. F. Motivated forgetting: A failure to replicate Glucksberg and King. Unpublished manuscript, Walter Reed Army Institute of Research, Washington, D.C., 1969.

Hall, R. V., Lund, D., & Jackson, D. The effects of teacher attention on study behavior. *Journal of Applied Behavior Analysis,* 1968, **1,** 1–12.

Hansen, J. C., Niland, T. M., & Zani, L. P. Model reinforcement in group counseling with elementary school children. *Personnel and Guidance Journal,* 1969, **50,** 741–744.

Harlow, H. F. The development of learning in the rhesus monkey. *American Scientist,* 1959, **47,** 459–479.

Jensen, A. R. *Understanding readiness: An occasional paper.* Urbana, Ill.: ERIC Clearinghouse on Early Childhood Education, 1969.

Johnston, J. M., & Pennypacker, H. S. A behavioral approach to college teaching. *American Psychologist,* 1971, **26,** 219–244.

Keller, F. S. Goodbye, teacher. . . . *Journal of Applied Behavior Analysis,* 1968, **1,** 79–90.

Mowrer, O. H. *Learning theory and behavior.* New York: Wiley, 1960.

Neill, A. S. *Summerhill.* New York: Hart, 1960.

Pavlov, I. P. *Conditioned reflexes* (translated by G. V. Anrep). Oxford: Oxford University Press, 1927.

Premack, D. Toward empirical behavior laws: 1. Positive reinforcement. *Psychological Review,* 1959, **66,** 219–233.

Price, P. Ninth graders to teach ecology to fifth graders and themselves. *Buffalo Evening News,* November 11, 1970.

Pronko, N. H. On learning to play the violin at the age of four without tears. *Psychology Today,* 1969, **2**(12), 52–53, 66.

Pryor, K. The porpoise caper. *Psychology Today,* 1969, **3**(7), 47–48, 64.

Reese, E. P. *The analysis of human operant behavior.* Dubuque, Iowa: Brown, 1966.

Rosen, S. Pianists on piano lessons—A parent's guide. *Bravo,* 1971, **10**(3), 6–8, 23, 24.

Skinner, B. F. *The behavior of organisms.* New York: Appleton-Century-Crofts, 1938.

Spencer, R. J. An empirical study of elementary teachers' attention as reinforcement for student behavior. Unpublished doctoral dissertation, Department of Educational Psychology, State University of New York at Buffalo, 1972.

Thomas, D. R., Becker, W. C., & Armstrong, M. Production and elimination of disruptive classroom behavior by systematically varying teacher's behavior. *Journal of Applied Behavior Analysis,* 1968, **1,** 35–45.

Torrance, E. P. *Encouraging creativity in the classroom.* Dubuque, Iowa: Brown, 1970.

Warner, R. W., Jr., & Hansen, J. C. Verbal-reinforcement and model-reinforcement group counseling with alienated students. *Journal of Counseling, Psychology,* 1970, **17,** 168–172.

Watson, J. B., & Rayner, R. Conditioned emotional reactions. *Journal of Experimental Psychology,* 1920, **3,** 1–14.

Weisberg, P., & Waldrop, P. B. Fixed-interval work habits of Congress. *Journal of Applied Behavior Analysis,* 1972, **5,** 93–97.

Zabranskey, M. L. Punishment for gum chewing had become a reinforcement for gum chewing. Unpublished course paper, State University of New York at Buffalo, December 21, 1970.

AUTHOR INDEX

SUBJECT INDEX